Reading Comprehension Across the Genres

Grade 6

MW01286254

Contents

Reading Comprehension Across the Genres

A Simple, Flexible Solution for Reading Skills Support

Homework

Assign meaningful, student-centered homework that can be completed in a single sitting.

Practice

Assign independent practice for core reading skills.

Remediation

Target certain text types or skills that need further attention.

Reinforcement/ Review

Support and review key topics from your curriculum.

Enrichment

Provide students with opportunities for deeper study.

Reading Comprehension Across the Genres 6, SV1419023616

Core Reading Skills Instruction

Reading Comprehension Across the Genres provides activity-based instruction for the reading skills that matter most, including . . .

- Identifying main idea and supporting details
- Analyzing author's purpose
- Making inferences
- Drawing conclusions
- Understanding a text's key features
- Making connections to other texts and to the real world
- Extending the text into writing and speaking

Wide Exposure to Genres

Reading Comprehension Across the Genres helps students master core reading skills while providing important exposure to a wide **variety of genres, or text types**, including . . .

- essays
- novels
- letters
- reviews

- cartoons
- poems
- scripts
- journals

- short stories
- advertisements
- functional documents
- tables and charts

Clear, Student-Friendly Lessons

Each lesson in *Reading Comprehension Across the Genres* begins with a **short reading selection** followed by **five exercises**.

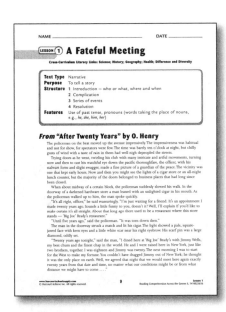

Before Reading

Students are introduced to the important aspects of the text, including its type, purpose, structure, and core features.

After Reading

Students complete five exercises that provide careful, student-friendly guidance in understanding the text.

5-Step Exercise Format

The carefully designed exercise format guides students step-by-step through the lessons—taking students from basic understanding to complete comprehension!

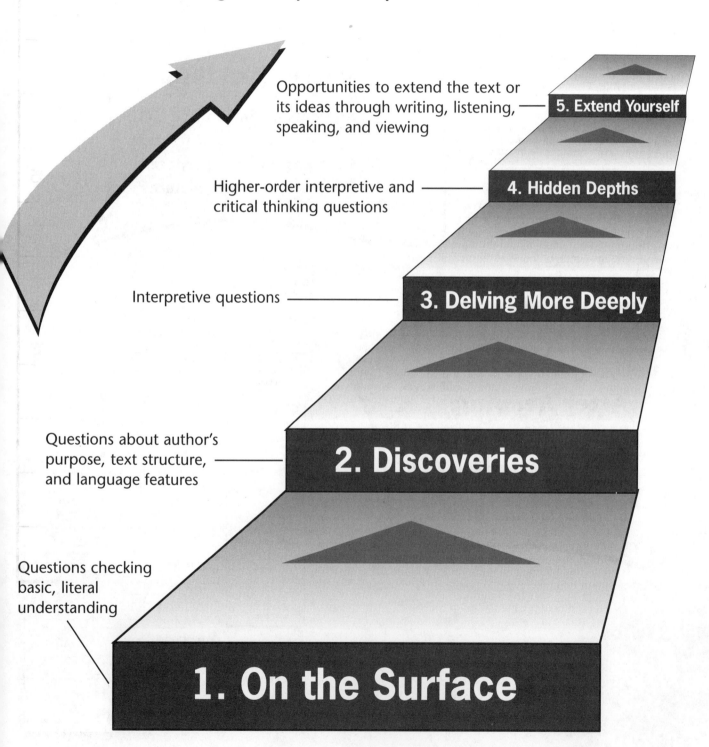

Opportunities to extend the text or its ideas through writing, listening, speaking, and viewing — **5. Extend Yourself**

Higher-order interpretive and critical thinking questions — **4. Hidden Depths**

Interpretive questions — **3. Delving More Deeply**

Questions about author's purpose, text structure, and language features — **2. Discoveries**

Questions checking basic, literal understanding — **1. On the Surface**

Correlation to Genres

Genre or Text Type	Lesson
Informative Nonfiction	8, 12, 14, 17, 20, 24, 25
Narrative Fiction	1, 9, 18, 27
Persuasive/Analytical Documents	11, 22, 30
Functional Documents	5, 7, 10, 15, 16, 19, 21, 26, 29, 32, 34, 35
Formal Letters	4, 33
Informal Letters	4
E-Communications	28
Poetry	13
Scripts/Dramas	6, 31
Journals	2, 3
Cartoons	23

Cross-Curriculum Literacy Links

Curriculum Area	Lesson
Arts	5, 6, 8, 9, 13, 18, 19, 21, 23, 29, 32, 33, 34
Civics and Citizenship	6, 13, 15, 17, 22, 23, 27, 28, 33, 34
Difference and Diversity	1, 3, 15, 18, 23, 24, 25, 27, 35
Drama	29, 30, 31
Geography	1, 2, 3, 6, 8, 14, 15, 16, 17, 20, 21, 22, 27, 28
Health	1, 3, 4, 16, 17, 18, 19, 20, 21, 22, 24, 25, 28, 32, 33, 34, 35
History	1, 2, 4, 5, 6, 10, 11, 12, 13, 14, 17, 18, 20, 21, 22, 23, 27, 28
Mathematics	2, 16, 17, 21, 24, 26
Multicultural Content	12, 15, 16, 23, 27
Science	1, 5, 7, 8, 9, 11, 12, 16, 17, 19, 20, 21, 22, 24, 25, 28, 34, 35
Work, Employment, and Enterprise	4, 11, 12, 17, 18, 19, 24, 25, 28, 32, 33, 34

Reading Comprehension Across the Genres 6, SV1419023616

LESSON 1 A Fateful Meeting

Cross-Curriculum Literacy Links: Science; History; Geography; Health; Difference and Diversity

Text Type	Narrative
Purpose	To tell a story
Structure	1 Introduction — who or what, where and when
	2 Complication
	3 Series of events
	4 Resolution
Features	Use of past tense, pronouns (words taking the place of nouns, e.g., *he, she, him, her*)

From "After Twenty Years" by O. Henry

The policeman on the beat moved up the avenue impressively. The impressiveness was habitual and not for show, for spectators were few. The time was barely ten o'clock at night, but chilly gusts of wind with a taste of rain in them had well nigh depeopled the streets.

Trying doors as he went, twirling his club with many intricate and artful movements, turning now and then to cast his watchful eye down the pacific thoroughfare, the officer, with his stalwart form and slight swagger, made a fine picture of a guardian of the peace. The vicinity was one that kept early hours. Now and then you might see the lights of a cigar store or an all-night lunch counter, but the majority of the doors belonged to business places that had long since been closed.

When about midway of a certain block, the policeman suddenly slowed his walk. In the doorway of a darkened hardware store a man leaned with an unlighted cigar in his mouth. As the policeman walked up to him, the man spoke quickly.

"It's all right, officer," he said reassuringly. "I'm just waiting for a friend. It's an appointment I made twenty years ago. Sounds a little funny to you, doesn't it? Well, I'll explain if you'd like to make certain it's all straight. About that long ago there used to be a restaurant where this store stands — 'Big Joe' Brady's restaurant."

"Until five years ago," said the policeman. "It was torn down then."

The man in the doorway struck a match and lit his cigar. The light showed a pale, square-jawed face with keen eyes and a little white scar near his right eyebrow. His scarf pin was a large diamond, oddly set.

"Twenty years ago tonight," said the man, "I dined here at 'Big Joe' Brady's with Jimmy Wells, my best chum and the finest chap in the world. He and I were raised here in New York, just like two brothers, together. I was eighteen and Jimmy was twenty. The next morning I was to start for the West to make my fortune. You couldn't have dragged Jimmy out of New York; he thought it was the only place on earth. Well, we agreed that night that we would meet here again exactly twenty years from that date and time, no matter what our conditions might be or from what distance we might have to come . . . ."

On the Surface

1 Name the two main characters in the passage from "After Twenty Years."

_____

2 What is noteworthy about the waiting man's appearance?

_____

3 How long has it been since the waiting man was in New York? _____

4 Describe the setting where the man waits.

_____

5 What is the man waiting for? _____

Discoveries

1 Refer to a dictionary; then write definitions for the following words as they are used in this text.

   a intricate _____   **c** stalwart _____

   b pacific _____   **d** swagger _____

2 Write synonyms (words with the same or similar meanings) for these words as they are used in this text.

   a depeopled _____   **c** vicinity _____

   b thoroughfare _____

3 List five examples, from this text, of verbs that describe actions that occurred in the past.

_____

Delving More Deeply

1 This text is part of the introductory section of a narrative or story. What information does it provide about the two characters?

_____

_____

_____

2 Why does the man quickly tell the officer the reason he is waiting in the doorway?

_____

3 Why didn't Jimmy Wells go West to make his fortune, too?

_____

4 What do the scar and the large diamond suggest about the man's past?

_____

_____

5 What actions does the police officer take that show his ability to do his job?

_____

_____

_____

Hidden Depths

1 "After Twenty Years" is set early in the twentieth century. What does this tell you about the trip from the West back to New York and the man who made it?

_____

_____

_____

2 What do you predict will happen as the man waits — will Jimmy show?

_____

_____

Extend Yourself

- Write the rest of the short story, based on what you have read and what you predict will happen. Share your story with your classmates.

- Find a copy of "After Twenty Years" and finish the story. Compare your ending to O. Henry's.

- New York City has inspired a lot of art. Find paintings or photographs of New York from around 1900, and discuss how they illustrate the story's setting.

- What are the rules for keeping appointments in our culture? Must one be on time? Can one be "fashionably late"? Check the rules in several etiquette books and report your findings to the class.

NAME _____   DATE _____

Land Ahoy

Cross-Curriculum Literacy Links: Geography; History; Mathematics

Text Type Journal

Purpose To reconstruct past experiences by retelling events in the order in which they occurred

Structure 1 Introduction — background information about who, where, and when

2 Series of events in chronological order

3 A personal comment (optional)

Features Abbreviations, informal language, varied sentences, personal reflections

From The Mahogany Ship

Time	Lat.	South	Long.	East	Observation
1543 Aug 15 noon	37	1	149	58	W.N.W. Fresh gales and cloudy. A heavy sea from the westward. A great many seabirds in sight, unnaturally active. Land distant with dark hills close to shore.
16	38	3	149	49	W.N.W. Moderate breeze, and cloudy. Sounded in ninety fathoms, no ground. Distance from the nearest shore about five miles. Land steep with many headlands.
17	38	30	148	01	N.N.E. Moderate breeze, hazy. Saw a number of whales, spouting. Very quiet. Crew unsettled. Land low and dark, hills falling away to the land. Unusual vegetation. Sounded in ninety fathoms, broken shells and sand which we sifted.
18	39	15	147	28	Variable. Light breeze, and clear. Sighted singular peak some way inland. Passed through a spot of yellow colored water. Saw smoke from fires on land. Crew uneasy.
19	39	57	146	40	Variable. Misty. A current to the southward. Made for land, anchored in an open bay with small islands. No seabirds. Unusual scent from vegetation. Very quiet. Prepared boats with much apprehension. Prayed.

"The Mahogany Ship" by Liam Davison. *The Second Largest Island: Modern Australian Short Stories*, Ed. Belinda Rickard Bell. Maryborough: Flinders Publishing, 1994. p. 84.

On the Surface

1   At what time was the first entry made?

_____

2   How many days does the journal cover?

_____

3   Explain how the weather changes during this time.

_____

4   What distance is the ship from the nearest shore by 16 August?

_____

5   With what feeling did the sailors prepare the boats?

_____

Discoveries

1   Write the meanings of the following words.

   a apprehension _____

   b gale _____

   c fathom _____

   d headland _____

2   List the topics at the top of each column in the journal.

_____

3   The ship is in Latitude South, Longitude East. Locate the position of the ship on a map and answer the questions below.

   a Is the ship north or south of the equator? _____.

   b Is the ship east or west of the prime meridian (the prime meridian runs through Greenwich, England)? _____.

Delving More Deeply

1 Who do you think is writing this journal?

_____

2 What indicates the ship is close to land?

_____

3 As the ship gets closer to shore, it "sounds." Explain what this means.

_____

4 Have the sailors been to this land before? How do you know?

_____

5 Is the land inhabited? How do you know?

_____

Hidden Depths

1 How are the sailors feeling about landing? Outline what you believe they are thinking.

_____

2 Have you ever been to a place you were unfamiliar with? Describe the unusual sights, smells, and sounds.

_____

_____

Extend Yourself

- On a map, trace the journey of the ship following the latitude and longitude mentioned in the journal. Where did the Mahogany Ship anchor? Find out more about the Mahogany Ship. Write a brief report on your findings.

- Write a journal entry from the point of view of one of the sailors.

- Discuss the purpose of the captain's log. How is it like the purpose of the black box on airplanes?

- What do you think motivates people to travel into the unknown? In the library, research famous discoverers. Write a report on what they discovered and present your findings to the class.

- Study a famous shipwreck through online sources.

LESSON 3 School Camp

Cross-Curriculum Literacy Links: Geography; Health; Difference and Diversity

Text Type   Account

Purpose   To reconstruct past experiences by retelling events in the order in which they occurred

Structure   1 Introduction — background information about who, where, and when

2 Series of events in chronological order

3 A personal comment (optional)

Features   Uses past tense, action verbs, descriptive language, may include quotes

Camp Scorcher

We set off for Camp Scorcher on Monday morning. We were due to leave at 9 A.M. but it took ages to pack all the gear into the bus so we were 20 minutes late.

We arrived at Camp Scorcher at about 2 P.M. and were shown where our huts were. I was in Hut 4.

After we unpacked we had "orientation" — lots of talk and rules. Then we had free time, dinner (burgers), and a night walk. It was fun but a bit scary walking in the woods at night. We saw a raccoon and a few possums and millions of trees.

Tuesday was a scorcher — so hot the road started to melt and get sticky! We did activities from a roster. It was our turn for archery, raft building and low ropes. Our raft collapsed! At night we had a BBQ and told stories around the campfire.

On Wednesday we did high ropes, canoeing, and horseback riding. We swam most of the afternoon because it was still scorching. Dinner was chicken and salad. After dinner we worked on our comedy skit for "Limelight Night."

Thursday we did the challenge course. Our hut came 2nd by 17 seconds. We made up for it by winning "Limelight" though. Our skit was hilarious. Dinner was Spag.

On Friday we had to clean up the huts, pack up our gear, and have a presentation of awards. I got a certificate of participation and a chocolate bar for being in the winning hut for "Limelight."

The bus trip home was long and boring. We were all tired and a bit sad to be going back to normal life after such a great week together.

Camp Scorcher was fun and it certainly lived up to its name.

On the Surface

1   Which camp did the student attend? _____

2   How long was the student at the camp? _____

3   What type of vehicle was used to transport the students to camp? _____

4   What main meals were served at camp?

_____

_____

5   List the activities available to students at this camp.

_____

_____

_____

Discoveries

1   Find the meanings of the following.

   a   scorcher _____   **b**   skit _____

2   Underline and discuss examples of informal language (everyday, colloquial, or personal language) and abbreviation used in this text.

3   Find words referring to the time sequence in this text.

_____

_____

_____

4   Locate examples of exaggerated language, or hyperbole, in this text. (e.g., "hilarious")

_____

5   Using the information in this text, complete the following table.

Day	Activities	Main meal
Monday	Orientation, night walk	

Delving More Deeply

1   Which activities do you think the student enjoyed most at camp? Why?

_____

2   What do you think the student meant by "it certainly lived up to its name"?

_____

3   Why did the students have to participate in "Limelight"? _____

_____

4   Do you think this student is competitive? Give evidence.

_____

_____

5   Why do you think the students were feeling tired and sad on their way back to school at the end of the camp?

_____

_____

Hidden Depths

1   What do students learn by going to camp? Circle the answer.

   a Independence   d How to tackle challenges

   b Cooperation   e All of the above

   c Tolerance

2   This student had a "great week." How do you think a shy, studious student would have felt about this camp experience and why?

_____

_____

Extend Yourself

•   Draw an imaginary map of Camp Scorcher. Show the location of buildings and activities.

•   Camp Scorcher is focused on physical challenges and does not seem to account for students who, for example, are shy or unathletic. With a partner, discuss how this focus might exclude some students. Then create a more inclusive and varied program of activities and meals for Camp Everybody.

LESSON (4) Dear Friend

Cross-Curriculum Literacy Links: History; Health; Work, Employment, and Enterprise

Text Type	Letters, transactional texts
Purpose	To communicate information, experiences, or ideas (formally or informally) to a reader who is not present
Structure	1 Address and date
	2 Greeting or salutation
	3 Series of events or issues in paragraphs
	4 Sign off
Features	Set layout, informal or formal language depending on purpose and audience, varied sentences

Formal and Informal Letters

Cityside Secondary College
42-54 South Street
Riverton, IL 12987

February 15, 2004

Re: School Camp, Sixth Grade

Dear Parent/Guardian,

   As you will recall from our Information Night and the School Newsletter, Grade 6 students will be attending Camp Scorcher from Monday to Friday of next week. This outdoor education opportunity is an important part of the school's program for your child's overall development, and all students are expected to attend. Trained camp personnel will supervise your child at Camp Scorcher, assisted by school staff.

   A permission form, medical information form, and list of items required by students accompany this letter. Please complete and return the forms promptly to the school office.

   If you experience difficulty in locating or providing any items of camp equipment, please contact your child's homeroom teacher immediately.

   Thank you for your cooperation and support in this matter.

Yours sincerely,

Francine

Ms. Francine Price
Grade 6 Coordinator

Camp Scorcher

Wed 6/9/2004

Dear Mom,

Camp is great. I thought I'd hate it at first but it's turned out to be fun. Kim is in my hut, so I'm not just with people I don't know. Anyway, we all know each other now — do we ever!

We've been canoeing, climbing, low ropes and HIGH ropes, hiking in the woods, and doing lots of swimming.

The food is OK — NOT as good as yours — but plenty of it.

I've got to go. We have to rehearse our skit — again!

See you soon!

Love, Sam

On the Surface

1 Who wrote the first letter? _____

2 Who will read and respond to the first letter?

_____

3 Who will supervise the students at Camp Scorcher?

_____

4 Who wrote the second letter? _____

5 Where was the second letter written? _____

Discoveries

1 Find the meanings of the following words as they are used in the text.

   a personnel _____   b guardian _____

2 Underline all the proper nouns (specific names of a person, place, or thing) in the first letter.

_____

3 Highlight words in the first letter that you can replace with simpler words to make the letter easier to read. Write your "plain English" alternatives above the highlighted words. Discuss the changes (e.g., recall = remember).

Delving More Deeply

1 What is the purpose of the first letter? Circle the answer.

    a To inform

    b To gain permission

    c To gain medical information

    d All of the above

2 How many attachments are included with the first letter? _____

3 Is school camp optional? Give evidence to support your answer.

_____

4 Has Sam's opinion of camp changed? If so, how?

_____

5 Has Sam made new friends at camp? Justify your answer.

_____

Hidden Depths

1 Which letter is formal and which is informal? List differences in purpose, audience, and language to support your view.

_____

_____

_____

2 Would Sam expect to get a written reply? Why or why not?

_____

Extend Yourself

- Collect letters as a class or group and classify them as formal or informal.

- Many companies now have a "plain English" policy. Why would this be? Examine some formal letters and see if you can find examples of "plain English."

- Rewrite Sam's letter as an e-mail or phone conversation. Are these text forms more or less formal than Sam's letter? Why?

- Locate some letters written by famous people. Give an introduction; then read them aloud as a dramatic presentation to your class.

LESSON ⑤ Understanding the Dictionary

Cross-Curriculum Literacy Links: Science; History; Arts

Text Type Dictionary
Purpose To give the meaning, pronunciation, grammatical use, and history of words in a language
Structure
1 Headword		5 Phrases and compounds
2 Pronunciation		6 Derivatives
3 Part of speech		7 Cross-references
4 Definitions		8 Etymology, or word origin

Features Abbreviations, font changes

HEART   1. *Anatomy* **a.** The chambered muscular organ in vertebrates that pumps blood received from the veins into the arteries, thereby maintaining the flow of blood through the entire circulatory system. **b.** A similarly functioning structure in invertebrates. **2.** The area that is the approximate location of the heart in the body; the breast. **3a.** The vital center and source of one's being, emotions, and sensibilities. **b.** The repository of one's deepest and sincerest feelings and beliefs: *an appeal from the heart; a subject dear to her heart.* **c.** The seat of the intellect or imagination: *the worst atrocities the human heart could devise.* **4a.** Emotional constitution, basic disposition, or character: *a man after my own heart.* **b.** One's prevailing mood or current inclination: *We were light of heart.* **5a.** Capacity for sympathy or generosity; compassion: *a leader who seems to have no heart.* **b.** Love; affection: *The child won my heart.* **6a.** Courage; resolution; fortitude: *The soldiers lost heart and retreated.* **b.** The firmness of will or the callousness required to carry out an unpleasant task or responsibility: *hadn't the heart to send them away without food.* **7.** A person esteemed or admired as lovable, loyal, or courageous: *a dear heart.* **8a.** The central or innermost physical part of a place or region: *the heart of the financial district.* See synonyms at **center. b.** The core of a plant, fruit, or vegetable: *hearts of palm.* **9.** The most important or essential part: *get to the heart of the matter.* **10.** A conventional two-lobed representation of the heart, usually colored red or pink. **11.** *Games* **a.** A red, heart-shaped figure on certain playing cards. **b.** A playing card with this figure. **c. hearts** (*used with a sing. or pl. verb*) The suit of cards represented by this figure. **d.** A card game in which the object is either to avoid hearts when taking tricks or to take all the hearts. **at heart** In one's deepest feelings; fundamentally. **by heart** Learned by rote; memorized word for word. **do (one's) heart good** To lift one's spirits; make one happy. **from the bottom (or depths) of (one's) heart** With the deepest appreciation; most sincerely. **have (one's) heart in (one's) mouth** To be extremely frightened or anxious. **have (one's) heart in the right place** To be well-intentioned. **heart and soul** Completely; entirely. **in (one's) heart of hearts** In the seat of one's truest feelings. **lose (one's) heart to** To fall in love with. **near (or close to) (one's) heart** Loved by or important to one. **steal (someone's) heart** To win one's affection or love. **take to heart** To take seriously and be affected or troubled by: *Don't take my criticism to heart.* . . .

from *The American Heritage® Dictionary of the English Language.* 4th Ed. 2000.

On the Surface

1   What is the first meaning of the word *heart* listed in this dictionary entry?

_____

2   How many main meanings of the word *heart* are shown here?

_____

3   Draw a picture of a heart as described in meaning 10.

_____

4   What color is the hearts suit in playing cards? _____

5   We sometimes call the center of a city the _____ of a city.

Discoveries

1   The word *heart* is derived from, or has its origin in, Old English, which was spoken centuries ago. Find five more words in your dictionary that show the word origin. Write down the words and their origins.

_____

2   As a class, discuss the way that many languages have contributed to our modern English language. Why has the English language developed in this way?

Delving More Deeply

1   Name something you have learned "by heart."

_____

2   Name something that is "near to your heart."

_____

3   How would smokers act if they "took to heart" health warnings about smoking cigarettes?

_____

4   Why do we use the phrase "break a person's heart" when this isn't really possible?

_____

_____

5 Where do we usually use the word *sincerely?* Circle the answer.

    a At the end of informal letters

    b At the end of e-mails

    c At the end of formal letters

Hidden Depths

1 Why is the dictionary entry abbreviated and laid out in this fashion? Write *true* or *false.*

    a To look interesting _____

    b To save space _____

    c To be efficient _____

    d To confuse school students _____

2 Invent a new phrase using the word *heart.* Put your phrase into two sentences and see if your partner can guess its meaning.

Extend Yourself

• Why has the heart come to symbolize love? Do some research to trace the origins of this use of the word *heart.*

• Find two different dictionaries and look up their entries for the word *heart.* Compare the style of the dictionaries, the information provided, and the proposed audience for the dictionaries. Which of the three dictionary entries is most useful and why?

• Make a dictionary collection in your classroom.

LESSON (6) Dialogue

Cross-Curriculum Literacy Links: History; Geography; Arts; Civics and Citizenship

Text Type	Narrative, script
Purpose	To entertain, to make a social comment
Structure	1 Introduction — who or what, where and when
	2 Complication
	3 Series of events
	4 Resolution
Features	Character names, direct speech (words actually spoken), stage directions

from "Surprise"

The Highway 60 Hair-n-Nail Depot (the present)

Libby: Hold still! I can't get your hair combed out with all this wiggling goin' on!

Sarah: Sorry.

Libby: Why are you so antsy today, anyway?

Sarah: I don't know — I've just got things on my mind.

Libby: Tell us, girlfriend, and we'll solve all your problems. And for goodness' sake, hold still! I'm jabbing myself with hairpins 'cause you keep squirmin'.

Sarah: Well, it's about Jake's birthday — it's Saturday.

Rebecca: [from *across the room, where she is sweeping*] Hey! Party time!

Sarah: No, see, that's the thing. I asked Jake what he wants to do to celebrate, and he said he doesn't want a party. He wants — what did he say — nothing big, just a little get-together with friends.

Rebecca: So, you're lucky — you're getting off cheap!

Sarah: I guess, Becca . . .

Libby: I hear a "but" coming. What's the problem, honey?

Sarah: Last year, Jake said he didn't want me to spend money on an expensive gift. So I didn't, and then we had a fight because he really wanted a new fishing rod and didn't tell me.

Libby: [with *hairpins in her mouth*] Umm.

Sarah: Took him a while to calm down, Lib. So what if he really wants a party this time, and he's just not comfortable telling me?

Rebecca: How many friends is he talking about at this "get-together"?

Sarah: I don't have any idea. That's what worries me.

Libby: I tell you what, girl. You need to throw a big party — invite all your friends —

Rebecca:	Including us!
Libby:	[with a glance at Rebecca to hush her up]
	— and cook out. Get him that fishing rod. But don't tell him! I know
	Jake — he loves a good surprise.
Sarah:	That's not what he asked for . . .
Libby:	Honey, if he doesn't like it, you can tell him it was my idea. Now,
	you're ready to sit under that hairdryer for a bit. You just sit and
	think about the look on his face when he shows up for the party!

On the Surface

1 Who are the three characters in this script?

_____

2 Where are the characters, and what are they doing?

_____

_____

3 Why can't Sarah hold still enough for Libby to do her job?

_____

4 What is Rebecca doing during the conversation?

_____

5 What does Libby advise Sarah to do?

_____

Discoveries

1 What nicknames do the characters use, and what does this use tell you about their relationship?

_____

_____

2 What does Libby mean when she says that Sarah is "antsy"?

_____

_____

_____

Reading Comprehension Across the Genres 6, SV1419023616

Delving More Deeply

1 Why does Sarah worry that a party won't make Jake happy?

_____

_____

2 What marks of punctuation show how unsure Sarah is about what to do?

_____

_____

3 Libby calls Sarah "honey" and "girlfriend." What do these pet names tell you?

_____

_____

4 What emotions are the three characters feeling and revealing in this scene?

   a Libby: _____

   b Sarah: _____

   c Rebecca: _____

Hidden Depths

1 Look closely at Libby's language. What do you notice about her speech, and how does it shape what you think of her as a character?

_____

_____

_____

2 How could you tell this is a script?

_____

Extend Yourself

• Write a companion scene for Jake and two buddies as they discuss his birthday and what he hopes Sarah will plan.

• Act out this scene in your class.

• Write a scene for later in the play, in which Jake arrives at his surprise party. Is Libby right about Jake? Share your scene with classmates.

NAME _____ DATE _____

Cross-Curriculum Literacy Link: Science

Text Type	Procedure
Purpose	To give instructions or show how something is accomplished through a series of steps
Structure	1 Opening statement of goal or aim
	2 Materials required named in order of use
	3 Series of steps listed in chronological order
Features	Logical sequence of steps, may use technical language and diagrams

Physical Weathering of Rocks

Learn how weathering affects rocks. Safety Instructions: Wear safety glasses during these experiments and follow normal laboratory safety rules.

1   Collect a small bottle with a screw top lid. Fill it to the brim with water. Screw the lid on tightly. Put the bottle into a plastic bag. Place it into the freezer and leave overnight. What happens?

2   Soak a fragment of shale in a pan of water for 20 minutes. Remove and test how easily the surface can be scratched. Then dry the shale by heating it gently on a sand tray. Test it for scratching again after it has cooled. Repeat the soaking and drying process if time permits. What do you notice?

3   Using tongs, heat a small piece of granite in the Bunsen burner flame until it is very hot. Then drop the heated rock into a small pan of cold water. Examine the rock for changes and examine any residue in the pan.

On the Surface

1   What is the title of these experiments?

_____

2   What safety precautions are recommended?

_____

3   How many experiments are suggested? _____

4   Which experiment will take the longest time to perform?

_____

5   Why do you need to use tongs in the third experiment?

_____

Discoveries

1   Find meanings for these words as they are used in this text.

   a   experiment _____

   b   safety _____

   c   brim _____

   d   fragment _____

   e   shale _____

   f   surface _____

   g   process _____

   h   residue _____

2   Underline or highlight the words and phrases which direct action or act as commands in this text. Share and discuss.

3   Discuss the style of the text with a partner. What type of language is being used and why is it appropriate here?

_____

_____

4   How could you improve this text for someone not familiar with science experiments?

_____

Delving More Deeply

1   Make a list of all the equipment you would need to perform all three experiments.

_____

_____

2   Why is the first experiment relevant when it doesn't involve using rocks? Fill in the gaps.

   When the water f _____ , the ice will expand and crack the

   b _____ in the same way that ice could c _____ rocks.

3   Why do you think these experiments use only fragments and small pieces of rock?

_____

_____

4   What conclusion might you draw from these experiments? Fill in the gaps.

I _____ , w _____, and h _____ cause

weathering of rocks in the natural environment.

5   How would diagrams of the experiment make these instructions clearer or easier to follow?

_____

_____

Hidden Depths

1   In which area of science would you expect to find these experiments? Why?

_____

_____

2   Construct a hypothesis (possible theory) for each of these three experiments. Discuss the hypotheses in class.

Hypothesis 1 _____

Hypothesis 2 _____

Hypothesis 3 _____

Extend Yourself

- Ask your science or geography teacher if you can carry out these experiments. Write a report on your findings.
- Find other examples of procedural texts, and compare and contrast their purposes and features.

LESSON (8) **More Science**

Cross-Curriculum Literacy Links: Science; Geography; Arts

Text Type	Explanation
Purpose	To inform, to explain how or why things are as they are, or how things work
Structure	1 A general statement
	2 Series of statements or events in chronological or logical order
	3 Concluding statement
Features	Logical sequence of details or ideas, may use headings, diagrams, and tables

Weathering and Erosion of Rocks

Introduction

We usually regard landforms as unchanging parts of our world. In fact, this is not the case. Landforms are constantly changing, but usually so slowly that we do not notice. A good example is the weathering and erosion of large rocks.

Weathering

If you look closely at a large rock, you may be able to see evidence of change. There may be a pile of small pieces or fragments of rock around its base. This change is probably the result of weathering.

Three main factors cause weathering. These factors are wind, water, and sun. The most important factor involved in weathering depends upon the location of the rock — whether it is in a cave, in a desert, on the seashore, or high in the mountains.

Erosion

Weathered fragments of rock are often moved away by water or wind. These fragments then settle where the water or wind speed slows down. The movement of weathered rock is called erosion. The settling out of the eroded rock is called deposition.

These three processes, weathering, erosion, and deposition, have had an enormous influence on the appearance of our landscape and will continue to do so.

On the Surface

1 What is the title of this explanatory text?

_____

2 How do we usually regard landforms?

_____

3   What evidence of change might you find near a large rock?

_____

4   Which three main factors cause weathering?

_____

5   What does erosion mean?

_____

Discoveries

1   List all the technical words, or words specific to this subject, that you can find in this text.

_____

2   Find examples of adjectives (which modify nouns) and adverbs (which modify verbs) in this text. Highlight the adjectives and underline the nouns they modify. Circle the adverbs and draw arrows to the verbs they modify.

_____

Delving More Deeply

1   Write an outline summary of this explanation of weathering and erosion.

_____

2   Why would the location of a rock be an important factor in how it is weathered?

_____

_____

3   Why do you think erosion might be a source of concern for farmers?

_____

4   Do you think our landscape will continue to change? If so, why?

_____

5   Name three types of written material where you might read this explanation.

_____

_____

Reading Comprehension Across the Genres 6, SV1419023616

Hidden Depths

1   This explanation is informative but still personal. Find examples of words or phrases that add warmth or increase personal involvement. Discuss this style and give reasons for its use here.

_____

_____

2   How could this explanation be improved? Explain your answer.

_____

_____

Extend Yourself

•   Collect pictures of weathering and erosion and make a class display.

•   Make a model or diorama showing an aspect of weathering or erosion.

•   In the space below, make a mind map or graphic organizer of the information in this explanatory text.

(LESSON 9) Meeting the Martians

Cross-Curriculum Literacy Links: Science; Arts

Text Type	Narrative, Science fiction
Purpose	To tell a story, incorporating scientific fact or theory
Structure	1 Introduction — who or what, where and when
	2 Complication
	3 Series of events
	4 Resolution
Features	Use of past tense, pronouns (words taking the place of nouns, e.g., *he, she, him, her*), technical or scientific language

From Life on Mars

The inner door slid upwards. There was a hiss, and the outer door opened. The noise of many voices and of strange unearthly music swelled from the platform. Their guide jumped out and stood, bowing deferentially.

For just a moment McKay hesitated on the threshold of this climax to adventure. Then the three explorers stepped out into Ahla, the subterranean capital of Mars.

As the Earthmen left the car which had sped them 2,000 miles to Ahla through the subterranean tunnels of Mars, McKay's eyes swept the crowd of men and women on the platform. There might have been a hundred Martians, all dressed in some form of Grecian garment. McKay read eager curiosity in their faces — also calmness and complete absence of hostility.

"It's going to be okay," he said to Sterling and Ross. "We've got a reception committee!"

The music and voices ceased as an elderly Martian stepped forward. McKay advanced to meet him, with his companions just behind. When the Earthmen bowed and placed their hands over their hearts, a quick look of pleasure lighted the Martian's face, and he repeated the gesture. At the same time, a soft, welcoming "Ah" swelled from the crowd.

The Martian held out a handsome jeweled chain, similar to the one he was wearing. McKay leaned down, and the dignitary hung it round his neck. Then, smiling warmly, he embraced the Earthman. The moment called for a token of goodwill in return. McKay wore a wrist watch, and he offered it now. The Martian seemed delighted and indicated that the Earthmen were to accompany him.

from "Life on Mars," by Werner von Braun, in *Space Movies*, ed. Peter Haining. London: Pan Books, 1998, p. 65.

On the Surface

1 Where is this narrative set?

_____

2 List all the characters in this text.

_____

3 How have the Earthmen traveled to this place?

_____

4 What are the Martians wearing?

_____

5 Why are the Earthmen in this situation? Circle the answer.

    a They are traders.

    b They are explorers.

    c They are diplomats.

    d They are soldiers.

Discoveries

1 Refer to a dictionary and write definitions for these words as they are used in the text.

    a unearthly _____

    b deferentially _____

    c threshold _____

    d Grecian _____

    e hostility _____

    f accompany _____

2 Use highlighters to indicate and label the four parts of narrative structure evident in this text: introduction, complication, series of events, and resolution.

Delving More Deeply

1 Why do you think this selection is considered to be science fiction?

_____

_____

2 What is the main idea of this excerpt?

_____

3 How do the Martians greet the explorers? Give examples.

_____

4 Why do McKay and the Martian leader exchange gifts? Find other examples of this custom in history or current affairs.

_____

_____

5 Why do you think the capital of Mars would be underground? Circle the likely reasons.

    a because the surface of Mars is too mountainous for habitation

    b because the Martians like digging

    c because the surface of Mars is uninhabitable

    d because the climate on Mars is extreme

Hidden Depths

1 Many features of this Martian encounter are Earth-like. Find examples and discuss them with a partner.

2 How do you think the Earthmen felt before and during this first encounter with Martians? Justify your answer.

_____

_____

Extend Yourself

- Collect descriptions and pictures of Martians from film and literature.
- View scenes from *Star Wars* films and note the range of alien life-forms and environments.
- Research life in space and UFOs. Write notes and make a short speech to the class.
- Rewrite this scene with hostile, rather than welcoming, Martians.
- Rewrite this scene with no Earth-like features. Share your work with a partner or the class.
- Draw or paint a scene from this narrative.
- Recreate this scene visually as a storyboard for a film version.

LESSON 10 Using a Thesaurus

Cross-Curriculum Literacy Links: History

Text Type Thesaurus
Purpose To aid the expression of ideas in writing, to increase vocabulary
Structure Alphabetical, slang and informal language included
Features Abbreviations, font changes

Thesaurus Excerpts

Method of use:

1 Select a word or phrase to investigate for alternative expressions.

2 Look up the selected word or phrase.

3 If the word is in CAPITALS, it is a main entry word. It is followed by a full list of associated words and phrases.

4 If the word is followed by an arrow and several numbered words, choose the one closest to the meaning you are seeking. Then, look up that word to find all the associated words.

5 Choose the word or expression that best suits your needs.

EXPLAIN *v* clarify, define, elucidate, explicate, expound, shed light on, throw light on, unfold; **interpret,** construe, deconstruct, make of, read, read between the lines, take, understand; **comment,** commentate, editorialize; illustrate, exemplify; **annotate,** edit, gloss, margin, pave

explain *v* ➔ **1** clarify **2** justify **3** solve

CLARIFY *v* clear, clear up, demystify, elucidate, rationalize, shed light on, speak for itself, speak plainly, throw light on; **explain,** amplify, bring home to, elaborate, explicate, expound, flesh out, illuminate, illumine, illustrate, set out, spell out; **decipher,** decode, decrypt, puzzle out, resolve, see, solve, unravel, unscramble, untangle; **annotate,** comment, interpret

clarify *v* ➔ **1** be transparent **2** explain **3** simplify

JUSTIFY *v* authorize, be a reason for, be an excuse for, explain, give the devil his due, plead ignorance, rationalize, set right, set the score right, vindicate, warrant; **excuse,** acquit, clear, exculpate, exonerate; **extenuate,** gloss over, make allowances, palliate, put a good face on, put in a good word for, speak up for, varnish over, whitewash

justify *v* ➔ **1** acquit **2** forgive **3** print **4** tidy

SOLVE *v* crack (*Colloq.*), deduce, explain, figure out, find the key to, get out, hammer out, puzzle out, thrash out, turn the scales, work out, zero in; **resolve,** clear up, conclude, extract, find; **answer a need,** meet a requirement, satisfy

solve *v* ➜ **1** clarify **2** translate

from *Macquarie Dictionary and Thesaurus.* New South Wales: Macquarie University, 1998. pp. 663, 586, 745, 886.

On the Surface

1 What is the purpose of a thesaurus?

_____

2 List the four main entry words shown here from the *Macquarie Thesaurus.*

_____

3 Which part of speech is each entry word?

_____

4 Why are some of the words in capitals?

_____

_____

5 What does "Colloq." mean?

_____

Discoveries

1 Write three sentences using each of the selected words — *clarify, justify,* and *solve* — clearly showing their different shades of meaning.

_____

_____

_____

2 Write one sentence in which *clarify, justify,* and *solve* can all be inserted meaningfully.

_____

Delving More Deeply

1 Explain the difference between commenting on an issue (e.g., "Cats make good pets for city dwellers") and illustrating your point.

_____

_____

2 What kind of films or TV shows might include dialogue using words from the "justify" entry?

_____

3 List some situations that may need to be "solved."

_____

_____

4 Write down an extenuating circumstance (an excuse or justification) for failing to complete an assignment.

_____

5 Some skin products claim to have clarifying effects. What does this mean and why would this term be used?

_____

_____

Hidden Depths

1 What do we mean when we say that someone is "reading between the lines"?

_____

_____

2 Which one of these four thesaurus words does not include an arrow pointing to any of the other three main entry words? Why is this the case?

_____

_____

Extend Yourself

- Share unfamiliar vocabulary from the thesaurus among the class or within groups. Students should try to create short conversations or role-plays using the new vocabulary appropriately.
- Create a Venn diagram showing the interrelationships between the starting words.
- Create word searches or crosswords using a thesaurus and share them with the class.

(LESSON 11) Computer Games

Cross-Curriculum Literacy Links: Science; History; Work, Employment, and Enterprise

Text Type	Response, book review
Purpose	To respond personally, giving details and opinions of a text
Structure	1 Context — background information on the text, information about author
	2 Description of the text (including characters and plot)
	3 Intended audience
	4 Concluding statement (judgment, opinion, or recommendation)
Features	Language may be formal or informal depending on purpose and audience; may include examples, quotes, publisher, price

Blast Masters

This slice of nostalgia about the evolution of computer games, writes Joshua Gliddon, will make your trigger-finger itch.

Computer games have always been about blasting your opponent. The first true game, SpaceWar, was developed in 1961 as a means of showing off the capabilities of MIT's racy new Digital Equipment Corporation PDP-1 minicomputer. The PDP looked a lot like something Apple computer would come up with today, with a vibrant color scheme and a super-cool circular monitor. But on the surface, the game couldn't be any further from the retina-searing splat fests of today.

SpaceWar developers, led by a guy called Steve "Slug" Russell, were good computer geeks, and being geeks they loved science fiction. In particular, they dug the space opera novels written by E. E. "Doc" Smith (best known for his *Lensman* series), which included epic space battles between warring factions.

The obvious way to show off the PDP was to write an application where two warring factions battled it out in space. Two players each controlled a ship using toggle switches and could fire up to 31 "missiles" at their opponent. If one of the missiles hit the opposing ship, it exploded.

The game inspired legions of imitators, right up to the Asteroids and Space Invaders eras of the 1970s. It also inspired Nolan Bushnell, the fellow who eventually went on to make—and lose—a fortune by founding the most famous computer game company of all: Atari.

There were computer games before SpaceWar, but they ran on specialized electronic devices hardwired to run one game only. True computer games, whether they're coin-operated arcade games, PC games, or console games such as Sony's PS2, run on general-purpose machines capable of being programmed for other purposes. The DEC PDP-1 was just such a machine, and so SpaceWar has the honor of being the seed that grew a globe-enveloping industry. An original version of SpaceWar, running in the Java environment, is available online from MIT, and it's still strangely addictive! (http://lcs.www.media.mit.edu/groups/el/projects/spacewar/)

High Score traces the evolution of the games industry; but it's also more than that. It's a store of memories from the people who were there at the time, including the authors, who were obviously Space Invaders fiends (with the rest of us) back in the 1970s. It's also a store of images, and a wellspring of nostalgia for those of us who honestly, truly believe that they don't make 'em like they used to (except for The Sims.

Now that's what I call a game!).

High Score! The Illustrated History of Electronic Games, by Rusel Demaria and Johnny L. Wilson, McGraw Hill/Osborne, $46.95

"Blast Masters" by Joshua Gliddon.
The Bulletin 29 October 2002. P. 96.

On the Surface

1 What is the title of the book being reviewed?

_____

2 Who wrote the book?

_____

3 Who wrote this book review?

_____

4 Where was this book review published?

_____

5 What is the book about?

_____

Discoveries

1 As a class, list all the technical terms you can find in this book review. Discuss the meaning and effect of these words.

2 According to the author, why were computer games before SpaceWar not considered "true computer games"?

_____

_____

Delving More Deeply

1 Does the author of the book review think this book is worth reading? Why or why not?

_____

2 Who would be the recommended audience for this book?

_____

_____

3 Which sections of a bookshop or library might this book be located in?

_____

4 Why was the first true computer game invented?

_____

_____

5 Why was the first game set in space?

_____

Hidden Depths

1 What connotations (implied or suggested meanings) does the term "computer geeks" carry?

_____

2 Why does this book review focus so much on the game SpaceWar?

_____

_____

_____

Extend Yourself

• Collect and compare book reviews from different sources — magazines, newspapers, the Internet, catalogues.

• Review two different books for two different audiences. Share and discuss in your class or group.

LESSON 12 A Lesson in History

Cross-Curriculum Literacy Links: Science; History; Work, Employment, and Enterprise; Multicultural Content

Text Type	Description
Purpose	To describe the characteristic features of a particular thing
Structure	1 Opening statement — introduction to the subject
	2 Characteristic features of the subject
	3 Concluding comment (optional)
Features	Details involving senses to assist reader to visualize a scene or event

Archaeology

Archaeology can be defined as the scientific study of any culture or civilization by the excavation and description of its remains. Archaeology supports the study of history by discovering primary sources of evidence, such as artifacts and bones, which provide information about people and events in the past.

Archaeology is like a giant jigsaw puzzle. It involves searching sites for remnants of the people of the past and the way they lived their lives. Archaeologists investigate places, objects, tools, and even trash.

Archaeologists use many resources to research places they are planning to excavate. Books, journals, maps, photographs, notes, museum exhibits, and Internet sites all assist archaeologists to decide where to dig and what to look for.

Some of the sites surveyed and excavated by archaeologists include buildings, ruins, campsites, caves, ships, rubbish dumps, fields, farms, and monuments. Many of the artifacts found by archaeologists were actually discarded, or thrown away, by earlier inhabitants. The rubbish of the past can be treasure to historians and archaeologists. Items that remain are those that have not decayed or decomposed, such as pottery, metal, bones, glass, and stone.

Archaeology is not just digging up the past. A great deal of time must be spent both before and after a "dig" in researching documents and maps. Once an artifact has been discovered, its location is noted. Then it must be measured and recorded in great detail. Finally, it is carefully stored for future research.

By putting all the available pieces of the puzzle together historians and archaeologists try to reconstruct the events of the past and discover how our ancestors lived.

On the Surface

1   What is archaeology? _____

_____

2   What other field of study does archaeology support? How?

_____

3   What do archaeologists investigate?

_____

4   Name some sites archaeologists might excavate.

_____

_____

5   List some resources used by archaeologists for research.

_____

Discoveries

1   Define the following words.

    a   excavation _____

    b   artifact _____

    c   discarded _____

2   Underline and discuss the verbs or action words used in this text. How many of them are specific terms associated with this topic?

_____

3   Investigate the history or etymology of the word *archaeology*. List as many other "-ology" words as you can and investigate their histories as well.

_____

_____

Delving More Deeply

1   Why would archaeologists and historians be interested in trash or discarded items from the past? Circle the correct answer.

    a   Trash gives clues about how people lived.

    b   Trash provides information about what people ate.

    c   Trash can contain evidence of tools and materials from the past.

    d   All of the above

2 Why don't archaeologists study much wood, paper, or cloth?

_____

_____

3 List the three steps that take place after an artifact is discovered.

_____

4 What game or hobby is archaeology compared to here? Why?

_____

_____

5 What do historians and archaeologists do with the evidence or "pieces of the puzzle" they discover?

_____

Hidden Depths

1 What skills and characteristics would you need to be an archaeologist?

_____

_____

2 Many artifacts and bones are now returned to sites after study by archaeologists and historians. Why would this be done?

_____

_____

Extend Yourself

- Investigate the lives, work, and contribution of some famous archaeologists. Give a short talk to your class or group.

- On a United States map, mark some important archaeological sites. What evidence has been located at these sites? What does it teach us about the past?

- Read about the curse of the pharaohs' tombs. Do you believe there really was a curse? Why or why not?

 **LESSON 13** **My Grandfather**

Cross-Curriculum Literacy Links: History; Arts; Civics and Citizenship

Text Type	Poetry
Purpose	To entertain and express feelings or ideas
Structure	Varies from rhyming and rhythmic patterns to free form and verse
Features	Careful word choice for meaning and sound, repetition of words or sounds, use of imagery

"I Wish" by Judith Johnson

I wish I'd known my grandfather.
He gazes thoughtfully astute
from his portrait,
forever middle-aged,
in plump health.
I wish I'd known my grandfather.
My grandmother, widowed for thirty years,
worshipped his memory, his clothes
as he had left them,
suddenly, still in his drawers,
still warm with his living.
He gazes coolly analytical;
no doubt he had his faults
and foibles but his great talent
was his Dickens recitals
in the Town Hall at Christmas
for charity when people, it was said
wept and laughed, and wept and went
home in high spirits.
I wish I'd known my grandfather.
He must have been very warm, alive
and aware. I gaze at his portrait,
hanging beside a portrait
of Charles Dickens sent to him,
signed, from London.
My grandfather has gone.
The glass on the portrait
mirrors me,
sitting at the round cedar table,
writing.

In *200 Years of Australian Writing: An Anthology from the First Settlement to Today*,
ed. James F. H. Moore. Hobart: VDL Productions, 1997, p. 62.

NAME _____   DATE _____

On the Surface

1 The author wishes she had known her _____. This is emphasized by the repeated line:

_____

2 Write true or false after the following statements.

   a The man in the portrait was young. _____

   b The man in the portrait was middle-aged. _____

   c The man in the portrait was elderly. _____

3 How long was the grandmother a widow? _____

4 What was the grandfather's great talent?

_____

5 How is the grandfather described here?

_____

Discoveries

1 Discuss the meanings of the following words: *astute, analytical, alive,* and *aware.* Read the poem again, replacing these words with synonyms. Discuss why poets select words very carefully (think about sound as well as meaning).

2 What image or mental picture is presented to the reader at the end of the poem, and how does it link the author to her grandfather?

_____

_____

Delving More Deeply

1 How do we know the grandmother loved and missed her husband?

_____

2 Why did the grandfather give public performances? Circle the correct answer.

   a For charity

   b Because he liked performing

   c For money

   d Because he was famous for his skill

3 How do we know the recitals were popular and entertaining?

_____

_____

4 What was significant and special about the portrait hanging next to the one of the grandfather?

_____

5 Why didn't the author know her grandfather?

_____

Hidden Depths

1 Do you think the author has a realistic view of her grandfather? Why or why not?

_____

_____

2 Approximately when did the grandfather live, based on the information here?

_____

Extend Yourself

- Highlight or underline all the words used in the poem for their sound or precise meaning.
- As a class, arrange and hold a "Dickens Recital" or a recital of the works of American authors such as Langston Hughes and Katherine Paterson.
- Write an "I Wish" poem of your own, and supply a portrait to accompany it.
- Collect at least six poems you enjoy. Look up dictionary meanings for *alliteration* and *assonance*. Find and highlight examples of these poetic devices in your poetry collection.

LESSON 14 Australia's History

Cross-Curriculum Literacy Links: History; Geography

Text Type	Historical Report or Account
Purpose	To reconstruct past experiences by telling events in the order in which they occurred
Structure	1 Introduction — background information about who, where, and when
	2 Series of events in chronological order
	3 A personal comment (optional)
Features	Use of past tense, action verbs, descriptive language; may include quotes

Completing the Coastline

Although the shape of Australia was generally known when the British began settling at Sydney Cove, important bits of the outline were still a mystery. Was Australia in fact a continent? ...

The most interesting section of unknown coast was in the south, in the bottom right-hand corner. (The left-hand corner was well known; several ships had sailed part-way along the Great Australian Bight.)

A few people thought Van Diemen's Land (Tasmania) might be an island, and a naval surgeon, George Bass, was eager to discover if this were so. John Hunter had first sailed these waters ten years before, as Captain of *Sirius*. Now he was Governor in Sydney. The master of a ship recently wrecked off the Tasmanian coast told Governor Hunter that he was certain a strait existed. At the end of 1797, Hunter sent George Bass to find out.

The only available vessel was an open whaleboat. Bass sailed south with a crew of six. He found that the coastline did not continue straight down towards Tasmania, but began to curve inwards. At the southernmost point, which he named "Wilson's Promontory," Bass was astonished to find seven white men — starving, desperate convicts, marooned on a small island. They had escaped from Sydney in a stolen boat, with others, planning to find the recently wrecked ship and rob its cargo of rum. Unable to find the wreck, they just managed to reach the island. One night while the seven slept, the other convicts took the boat and sailed off.

George Bass and his crew got about halfway through the strait before they had to turn back, with a leaking boat and little food. They stopped again at the island, and took two of the convicts on board. The rest were ferried to the mainland. Bass gave them everything he could spare — a musket, half his ammunition, fishing hooks, a cooking pot, and showed them the direction to walk to Sydney, 800 kilometers away. They were never seen again.

George Bass was sure Tasmania was an island but he hadn't actually proved it. In October, 1798 he joined his friend, twenty-four-year-old Lieutenant Matthew Flinders, on board a small ship with orders from Governor Hunter to finish the task.

Flinders sailed the length of the strait, named it after Bass, and found it navigable by all sizes of ships, although the sea was rough, and there were dangerous islands. "Our long-wished-for discovery," said Flinders; "Mr. Bass and myself hailed it with joy." They then sailed around Tasmania. Now ships sailing to Sydney could cut through Bass Strait, saving days. A large island had been added to the map of the world.

from *The Ashton Scholastic History of Australia* by Manning Clark, Meredith Hooper & Susanne Ferrier.
Gosford: Ashton Scholastic, 1988, Ch. 8.

On the Surface

1 Which part of Australia was little known when the British began settling at Sydney Cove?

_____

2 What did John Hunter do before he became governor?

_____

3 What was George Bass's profession?

_____

4 On what mission did Governor Hunter send Bass in 1797?

_____

5 What sort of boat did Bass use for his first attempt?

_____

Discoveries

1 Use different colored highlighters to circle and label the three parts of historical account structure in this text — introduction, series of events in chronological order, and concluding comment. Share and discuss.

2 Underline past tense verbs in red, descriptive words or phrases in blue, and quotes (actual words spoken) in black. Share and discuss.

Delving More Deeply

1 Why was George Bass astonished to find the escaped convicts?

_____

_____

2 Why did the first attempt fail?

_____

www.harcourtschoolsupply.com   49   **Lesson 14**
Reading Comprehension Across the Genres 6, SV1419023616

3 Why do you think Bass assisted the escaped convicts? Should he have done so? What else could he have done?

_____

4 Why did Matthew Flinders accompany Bass on the second trip?

_____

5 Why was the strait named after Bass?

_____

_____

Hidden Depths

1 What sort of person do you think Bass must have been?

_____

2 How do you think Bass and Flinders felt after they had sailed the length of the strait?

_____

Extend Yourself

• Plot the two voyages of George Bass on a map of Australia.

• Write journal entries as if you were George Bass during these voyages.

• Hold a class discussion about who were the real discoverers of Australia.

• Read about the convict system or the reasons for British settlement in Australia and write a historical account.

LESSON (15) Map Reading

**Cross-Curriculum Literacy Links: Geography; Civics and Citizenship;
Difference and Diversity; Multicultural Content**

Text Type Map
Purpose To show locations and physical features
Structure 1 Pictorial representation of a region
2 Scale and orientation are often shown
Features Visual information, combining words, symbols, and images

The Continent of Australia

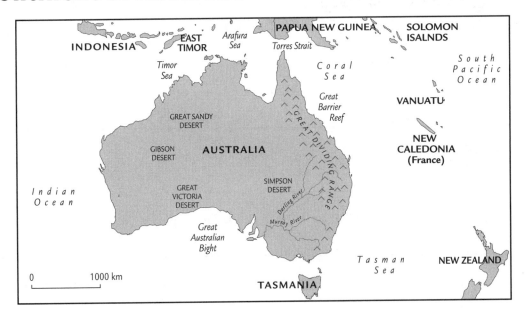

On the Surface

1 Name the continent shown on this map.

_____

2 Name the oceans and seas shown on this map.

_____

_____

3 How many deserts are shown here?

_____

4 What two rivers are shown on the map?

_____

5 What is the name of the mountain range along the east coast of Australia?

_____

Discoveries

1 What symbols are used to represent mountains and rivers?

_____

2 How many times is the word *great* used on this map and what does it mean?

_____

Delving More Deeply

1 Who are Australia's northern neighbors?

_____

2 Where could Australians go for a South Pacific Island holiday?

_____

3 What language would be spoken in New Caledonia? Why?

_____

4 What stretch of water separates Australia from Papua New Guinea?

_____

5 What evidence is there that the explorer Abel Tasman was influential in this region of the world?

_____

Hidden Depths

1 Why do you think the majority of Australia's population lives along its coastline?

_____

_____

_____

2 Compare this map to one of our continent. What differences strike you?

_____

_____

Extend Yourself

- Sketch this map yourself and label the significant features.
- Find early maps of Australia from the times of European discovery and compare their detail and assumptions.
- Use the Internet to find out how Europeans, especially the British, first came to Australia. Report your findings.
- Learn about the aboriginal peoples of Australia and their sacred places. Use a map and illustrations to create a poster or bulletin board of this information.

NAME _____   DATE _____

LESSON 16 Living and Dying

Cross-Curriculum Literacy Links: Mathematics; Science; Geography; Health; Multicultural Content

Text Type	Graph
Purpose	To visually display numerical information
Structure	Labeled *x* and *y* axes
	Visual or graphical representation of data
Features	May use average figures; scale can alter visual impact of information

2001 World Birth and Death Rates

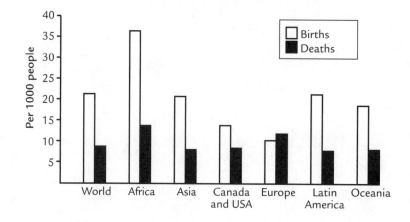

Demographers [people who study human population] use birth and death rates to determine population growth and evaluate the general health of the populations they study. These rates usually denote the number of births and deaths per 1,000 people in a given year, as in the chart above.

Estimates of world population before 1900 are based on scant evidence. However, scholars agree that, for most of humankind's existence, average population growth was approximately 0.0002% per year, or 20 per million inhabitants. This growth was not steady but dependent upon factors such as climate, food supply, natural disasters, disease and war.

The United Nations estimates that the world population reached 5.3 billion in 1990, and is increasing by more than 90 million people each year. This rate of increase, 1.7% per year, is below the peak rate of 2% per year reached by 1970, and is expected to continue to decline.

Encarta '96, Microsoft, 1993–5.

On the Surface

1 Why do demographers use birth and death rates?

_____

2 What does a birth or death rate per 1,000 people mean?

_____

_____

3 Which part of the world has the highest birth rate? _____

4 Which part of the world has the lowest birth rate? _____

5 What is the highest death rate, and where is it found?

_____

Discoveries

1 Find the meanings of the following words.

    a demographer _____

    b population _____

    c denote _____

2 What is the benefit of displaying information in graphical form as it is shown here?

_____

_____

3 Where else might you expect to see information displayed in graphs?

_____

Delving More Deeply

1 What do demographers do?

_____

_____

2 Compare and contrast the birth and death rates in North America and Latin America.

_____

3 If the rates for 2001 were to stay the same for years to come, which part of the world might experience a declining population?

_____

_____

4 Which countries would be described as Oceania? Consult a dictionary or other source.

_____

_____

_____

Hidden Depths

1 Which continents show birth and death rate trends most similar to the world population trends shown on the graph? Why?

_____

2 What are some of the possible consequences of increasing population growth on the world?

_____

_____

Extend Yourself

- Collect recent data for birth and death rates. Graph your data. Is the rate of population increase slowing as expected? Explain.

- Collect graphs from the newspaper for one week. What sort of information is displayed graphically?

- Plot the same data several times on graphs with different scales. How can data be made to seem more or less extreme when graphically displayed?

- Investigate causes of death in the different continents using the Internet. What do your findings reveal about living conditions in different places in the world?

LESSON (17) **People Everywhere**

Cross-Curriculum Literacy Links: Mathematics; Science; History; Geography; Health; Work, Employment, and Enterprise; Civics and Citizenship

Text type	Explanation
Purpose	To inform, to explain how or why things are as they are, or how things work
Structure	1 A general statement
	2 Series of statements or events in chronological or logical order
	3 Concluding statement
Features	Logical sequence of details or ideas; may use headings, diagrams, and tables

Population

The term *population* means the number of humans living in an area, such as a city, country, or continent, at any given time. The study of population is known as demography. Demographers study the composition, size, and distribution of populations; changes over time through births, deaths, and migration; and the causes and consequences of such changes. Such studies yield knowledge important for governments that must plan for housing, health, education, employment, social security, and preservation of the environment.

In the 17th century, great advances in agriculture, industry, scientific knowledge, medicine, and social organization spurred great growth in population. Inanimate energy gradually replaced animal and human labor. People slowly learned to control disease. Over a 300-year period, all continents saw a five-fold population increase — from about 500 million in 1650 to 2.5 billion in 1950. However, increases were most striking in regions where new technologies were applied.

Beginning around 1950, a new phase of population growth arose when disease and famine could be controlled even in areas that did not have high levels of literacy or technological development. This happened as a result of the low cost of importing vaccines, antibiotics, insecticides, and high-yielding varieties of seeds. With improvements in water supplies, waste disposal facilities, and transportation, crop harvests increased, and deaths from parasitic and infectious diseases decreased. Life expectancy at birth in most developing countries increased from about 35–40 years in 1950 to 61 years by 1990. This trend of increased life expectancy, along with improved infant mortality rates, has led to greater population pressure on limited resources in many developing nations.

On the Surface

1 What does *population* mean?

_____

2 Name three ways populations change.

_____

3 What factors led to an increase in world population in the 17th century?

_____

_____

4 How great an increase in world population was recorded between 1650 and 1950?

_____

5 What factors have influenced population increase since 1950?

_____

Discoveries

1 Find the meanings of the following words.

   a modify _____

   b inanimate _____

   c parasite _____

2 Find synonyms in the text for the following words.

   a make-up _____   **d** non-living _____

   b provide _____   **e** used _____

   c a little at a time _____

3 Is this text written using formal (or impersonal) or informal (casual or personal) language? Give examples and explain why this is so.

_____

_____

_____

Delving More Deeply

1   Why do you think improvements in agriculture would lead to increases in population?

_____

_____

2   Why would improvements in medicine increase population figures?

_____

_____

3   Why would improvements in water supplies and waste disposal lead to population increases?

_____

_____

4   How long could you expect to live, on average, if you were born in a developing country in 1950?

_____

5   Is increased population a good thing or a bad thing in developing countries? Why?

_____

Hidden Depths

1   How might the government use population studies to plan for the "preservation of the environment"?

_____

2   Give examples of "inanimate energy" sources that have replaced animals and humans.

_____

Extend Yourself

•   Graph the information provided in this text.

•   Write a three-step plan to reduce the death rate in a developing nation.

•   What can people in our nation do to increase life spans in developing nations?

LESSON 18 # An Unexpected Visitor

Cross-Curriculum Literacy Links: History; Health; Arts; Work, Employment,
and Enterprise; Difference and Diversity

Text Type	Narrative
Purpose	To tell a story
Structure	1 Introduction — who or what, where and when
	2 Complication
	3 Series of events
	4 Resolution
Features	Use of past tense, pronouns (words taking the place of nouns, e.g., *he, she, him, her*)

from "The Ambitious Guest"

One September night a family had gathered round their hearth, and piled it high with the driftwood of the mountain streams, the dry cones of the pine, and the splintered ruins of great trees that had come crashing down the precipice. Up the chimney roared the fire, and brightened the room with its broad blaze. The faces of the father and mother had a sober gladness; the children laughed; the eldest daughter was the image of Happiness at seventeen; and the aged grandmother, who sat knitting in the warmest place, was the image of Happiness grown old. They had found the "herb, heart's-ease," in the bleakest spot of all of New England. This family were situated in the Notch of the White Hills, where the wind was sharp throughout the year, and pitilessly cold in the winter, — giving their cottage all its fresh inclemency before it descended on the valley of the Saco. They dwelt in a cold spot and a dangerous one, for a mountain towered above their heads, so steep that stones would often rumble down its sides and startle them at midnight.

The daughter had just uttered some simple jest that filled them all with mirth, when the wind came through the Notch and seemed to pause before their cottage — rattling the door, with a sound of wailing and lamentation, before it passed into the valley. For a moment it saddened them, though there was nothing unusual in its tones. But the family were glad again when they perceived that the latch was lifted by some traveler, whose footsteps had been unheard amid the dreary blast which heralded his approach, and wailed as he was entering, and went moaning from the door.

from "The Ambitious Guest" by Nathaniel Hawthorne, in *The Short Story*, ed. Brander Matthews.
New York: American Book Company, New York, 1907.

On the Surface

1   Who lives in the cottage in the Notch?

2 What dangers does the cottage face, located where it is?

_____

3 What is the family doing on this Saturday night?

_____

_____

4 What event causes the family to be suddenly saddened?

_____

5 What happens at the end of the passage?

_____

Discoveries

1 Write definitions for these words as they are used in this text.

   a sober   _____

   b situated   _____

   c inclemency   _____

   d jest   _____

   e lamentation _____

   f dreary   _____

   g heralded   _____

2 List examples of words used in the past tense in this text.

_____

Delving More Deeply

1 How does the family react to the presence of the stranger at the door?

_____

2 What does Hawthorne mean when he says that the family had "found the 'herb, heart's ease'"?

_____

_____

3   What details does Hawthorne include to show the family's contentment?

_____

_____

_____

4   Why do you think the family continues to live in this dangerous location?

_____

_____

5   What do you think "the Saco," below the Notch in the valley, is? Why?

_____

Hidden Depths

1   Why isn't the family frightened by the appearance of a stranger at their door?

_____

_____

_____

2   What do you think will happen to the stranger after he joins the family around the fire?

_____

_____

Extend Yourself

•   Read the rest of "The Ambitious Guest," and discuss the ending with classmates. Does the ending surprise you?
•   Many cultures teach that the law of hospitality must be followed. Find out about the law of hospitality, and locate stories or myths about what happens when people honor it or violate it.

LESSON 19 Promises, Promises

Cross-Curriculum Literacy Links: Science; Health; Arts; Work, Employment, and Enterprise

Text Type	Advertisement
Purpose	To persuade by putting forward an argument or particular point of view, to sell a product
Structure (varies)	1 Images
	2 Written or spoken language
	3 Sensory appeal, e.g., color, shape, music
Features	May include images, facts and figures, logical reasoning, examples, and persuasive or emotional language

El Gatito Kitten Food

The Right Nutrition for the Right Age.

Your kitten is growing at a rapid rate. If she were human, she'd be entering college by the time she's two-and-a-half. It's up to you, her caregiver, to see she gets the proper diet for her to grow into a healthy adult cat. At El Gatito, we have developed a food that will address the special dietary needs of your kitten.

El Gatito kitten food has all the nutrients your kitten will need in the first six months of life. All the El Gatitio varieties contain the necessary phosphorous to calcium ratio to make them strong as well as the proteins and calories to make them digestible for her tiny stomach.

The responsibility is yours, the food is El Gatito

el Gatito

On the Surface

1   What product is being advertised? _____

2   What is the product's full name? _____

3   What is the purpose of the product advertised here?

_____

4   Which company makes this product? _____

5   What are the special ingredients in this product that differentiate it from other similar products?

_____

Discoveries

1   How many font styles and sizes are used in this advertisement? Why?

_____

_____

2   Would a photograph of the products themselves be more or less effective advertising? Why?

_____

_____

Delving More Deeply

1   What is the motto of the company which manufactures these products, and what does it suggest?

_____

_____

2   What phrase in the ad makes the same point as the motto?

_____

3   Why do you think the kitten's rapid rate of growth is mentioned?

_____

_____

4   Other than the right nutrients for growth, what benefits does El Gatito kitten food provide?

_____

_____

5 Discuss three ways this advertisement attempts to appeal to customers.

_____

_____

_____

Hidden Depths

1 El Gatito means "the little cat" or "the kitten" in Spanish. What effect does the product's non-English name have on the ad?

_____

2 Who would be the target audience for this advertisement and where might you expect to see the advertisement?

_____

_____

Extend Yourself

- Create your own advertisement for this product.

- Investigate the cost of this and other kitten products and present your information in a table.

- Find out why phosphorous and calcium are necessary to a kitten's healthy growth. Do people need these minerals, too, to grow strong?

- Create a TV or radio advertisement for an imaginary product, using persuasive language.

LESSON 20 Our Rainforests

Cross-Curriculum Literacy Links: Science; History; Geography; Health

Text Type	Argument or exposition
Purpose	To persuade by putting forward an argument or particular point of view
Structure	1 Point of view is stated
	2 Justifications of argument in a logical order
	3 Summing up of argument
Features	Includes facts and figures, logical reasoning, examples, and persuasive or emotional language

from Rainforest Action Network

The lungs of the planet, the pharmacy of the future—the rainforests of the world get lumbered with a lot of responsibility. But the plain fact is, these ancient ecosystems are essential for all life on earth.

Among the vital functions they perform: stabilizing the Earth's climate, preserving wildlife habitat, and maintaining soil productivity.

And yet, for all their value, the rainforests are an appallingly abused asset, badly in need of some radical help. It was with this in mind that Randy Hayes founded the Rainforest Action Network in 1985, with the stated mission to protect the Earth's rainforests and support the rights of their inhabitants through education, grassroots organizing, and non-violent direct action.

Since its launch, RAN has been a world leader in rainforest conservation. It has educated and mobilized consumers and community action groups throughout the United States, through means as diverse as student information packages, grassroots skills training, and websites. And RAN works alongside environmental and human rights groups in dozens more countries, offering financial support and networking services to indigenous and environmental activists seeking ecologically sustainable solutions within their own regions.

The strengths of RAN's grassroots activism were obvious from its first direct-action campaign in 1987. It organized a boycott of Burger King, which was importing cheap beef from tropical countries where rainforests were being stripped to provide pasture for cattle. When sales dropped 12 per cent during the boycott, Burger King cancelled $35 million worth of beef contracts in Central America and announced it would no longer buy beef from the rainforest.

The success of the Burger King boycott taught American citizens that, if their consumption patterns could contribute to problems in far-off rainforests, they could equally contribute to solutions, not just through their purchasing power but also through letter-writing and public non-violent demonstrations, turning concern into effective action.

from *Take It Personally* by Anita Roddick. London: HarperCollins, 2001, Pp. 170–171.

On the Surface

1   What organization is this article promoting? _____

2   What vital functions do rainforests perform?

_____

3   Who founded this organization?

_____

4   How long has this organization been operating?

_____

5   What did RAN's first successful action accomplish?

_____

Discoveries

1   Underline all the emotional or persuasive words and phrases used in this text. Discuss.

2   Does this article provide both sides of the rainforest issue? Why or why not?

_____

3   How might employees of the targeted companies feel about the activities of this organization? What actions might they take in response?

_____

_____

Delving More Deeply

1   What is the mission of this organization?

_____

2   What methods does this organization recommend and use to achieve its mission?

_____

3   What is a "grassroots" campaign?

_____

4   How could eating a hamburger damage a rainforest?

_____

5 What is a boycott?

_____

_____

Hidden Depths

1 Why do you think RAN chooses grassroots activism as its major tool for change?

_____

_____

2 What are some possible negative results of successful campaigns by this organization? Consider, for instance, the effect on employees of boycotted businesses.

_____

_____

Extend Yourself

• Write a newspaper report about another direct-action campaign.

• With two or three partners, explore an environmental issue from all sides. Gather information independently. Then, work together to agree on a plan for solving the issue. Present the plan to your class.

• Make a directory of Web sites with information on the issues raised in the article.

(LESSON 21) Quiz Time

Cross-Curriculum Literacy Links: Mathematics; Science; History; Geography; Health; Arts

Text Type	Procedure, instructions
Purpose	To give instructions or show how something is accomplished through a series of steps
Structure	1 Opening statement of goal or aim
	2 Materials required listed in order of use
	3 Series of steps listed in chronological order
Features	Logical sequence of steps, may use technical language and diagrams

Twenty Questions

Goal: To guess the name of an imagined object in 20 questions or fewer

Equipment: None

Players: Two or more, any ages

How to play:
- The player who is "it" thinks of an object and tells the other players whether it is animal, vegetable, mineral, or combined. This category is the only clue that can be given.
- The other players take turns to ask questions to try to work out what the imagined object must be.
- The player who is "it" may respond to the questions only with a "Yes" or "No."
- If a player guesses the object incorrectly, he or she is out of the game until the next round.
- There is a limit of 20 questions.
- If a player guesses the object correctly, she or he is "it" for the next round.
- If no player guesses the object correctly after 20 questions, the player who is "it" gets another turn and chooses another object.

Note: The categories are very broad. "Animal" includes people and animals and animal products, such as butter and wool; "vegetable" includes anything organic that is not animal, such as paper and olive oil; "mineral" means anything that has never been alive, such as a television or a glass.

Variations:
- The game can be played in reverse. One player leaves the room while the other players choose an object. When the player returns he or she has 20 questions to guess the object correctly.
- Extra categories can be added such as "abstract" (ideas and emotions).
- Categories and objects can be restricted to a field, such as sports, food, history, geography, or science.

On the Surface

1   What is this game called? _____

2   How many people can play this game? _____

3   What four categories can the chosen object fall into?

_____

_____

4   What happens if a player makes an incorrect guess?

_____

_____

5   What happens if no one guesses the object correctly?

_____

_____

Discoveries

1   Animal, mineral, and vegetable are used as broad technical terms for categories in this game. Write two sentences for each of these words showing broad (or general) and narrow (or specific) meanings.

_____

_____

2   List some words used to name categories of food.

_____

_____

3   Use colored highlighters to show the features of a procedure present in this text.

Delving More Deeply

1   What variation to the game is suggested?

_____

_____

2   When and where do you think this game might be played?

_____

_____

3   What knowledge or understanding would you need to play this game?

_____

_____

_____

4 Do you think this game is played often these days? Why or why not?

_____

_____

_____

5 What are some advantages and disadvantages of this game?

_____

Hidden Depths

1 What mental skills do guessing games such as "Twenty Questions" use?

_____

_____

2 Explain why games need to have rules.

_____

Extend Yourself

- Create variations of this game that could be used for different school subjects. Test and refine your new games with your classmates.

- Find out what parlor games are. Research parlor games other than "Twenty Questions" and create a class book of them.

- Brainstorm in a group and list all the different types of procedures you can recall. Share your findings with the class and present them using a graphic organizer such as a Venn diagram.

LESSON 22 Our World

Cross-Curriculum Literacy Links: Science; History; Geography; Health; Civics and Citizenship

Text Type	Debate or discussion
Purpose	To inform and persuade by presenting evidence and opinions about more than one side of an issue
Structure	1 Opening statement presenting the issue
	2 Arguments or evidence for different points of view
	3 Concluding recommendation
Features	Includes facts and figures, logical reasoning, examples, persuasive or emotive language

Is Humanity Running Out of Resources?

Many environmentalists warned that by the end of the 20th century the world would start to run out of important resources. They warned of the destruction of rainforests; the growing numbers of plants and animals becoming extinct; and the pollution of air, water, and soil.

Some people worried that a profit-oriented society had used up resources, destroyed the environment, and created poverty for many. These pessimists were concerned that progress would lead to the destruction of wealth-producing resources such as oil, minerals, timber, clean water, and air. According to this view, the world should expect to run out of these resources. Industrialization and a global economy would use them up. The solutions suggested to fix these man-made problems seemed too little and too late. The answer seemed to lie in strict governmental management of such activities and in reducing the common Western goal of "getting and spending."

Optimists disagreed. They claimed that the scarcity and destruction of resources was being exaggerated. After all, humans and other species had survived on Earth for tens of thousands of years, through extremes of climate change. Also, when people face a problem, they tend to come up with a solution. Human history is rich with examples of our ability to overcome and rise above difficulties. Through discovery and invention humans would, once again, conquer and prosper.

As the 21st century progresses, we will be able to judge whether the pessimists or optimists were correct in their view, or whether the answer lies in between.

On the Surface

1   Rewrite the title in your own words.

_____

2   What is a "profit-oriented society"?

_____

3   Name some basic natural resources.

_____

4   List three elements of life.

_____

5   How many points of view are expressed here?

_____

Discoveries

1   Draw a line to match the words in the first column to their synonyms in the second column.

   a pessimists   no longer existing

   b optimists   opinion

   c solutions   those who expect good

   d view   those who expect bad

   e extinct   answers

2   Where might you read this text?

_____

3   What is the tone of this text? Give examples.

_____

_____

Delving More Deeply

1   In which countries in the world might such debates be taking place? Why?

_____

_____

2 Explain the viewpoints being expressed here. Use your own words.

_____

_____

3 Why is one view considered pessimistic and the other optimistic?

_____

_____

_____

4 Create a table showing the arguments supporting the different points of view. Share and discuss.

Viewpoint 1	Viewpoint 2

5 Which point of view is more convincing? Justify your answer.

_____

_____

Hidden Depths

1 What sort of evidence could be used to further support the first viewpoint?

_____

_____

2 What sort of evidence could be used to further support the second viewpoint?

_____

_____

_____

Extend Yourself

- Hold a class debate on this issue.

- With a partner, rewrite this text for younger students. Discuss and make the changes required to simplify the language for a different audience.

- Create a pamphlet for one side of this issue. Consider your audience carefully when planning the words and images you will use.

- Write and perform one side of this issue as a speech. Do some research and include more evidence. Use persuasive language and gestures when presenting your speech.

LESSON 23 Laugh Out Loud

Cross-Curriculum Literacy Links: History; Arts; Civics and Citizenship; Difference and Diversity; Multicultural Content

Text Type	Cartoon
Purpose	To entertain and/or make a social comment
Structure	1 Image or series of images, usually in the form of line drawings
	2 Written or spoken language accompanying images
Features	Visual and language cues to convey meanings at multiple levels; may be related to current affairs or social issues

Teen Talk

PXT. Mom.

On the Surface

1   What is odd about the text of the speech bubbles in this cartoon?

_____

2   What are the teens in the cartoon doing?

_____

3   What do you think the teen on the left is saying?

_____

4   What do you think the other teens reply?

_____

_____

_____

5   What words in the cartoon are easily read?

_____

Discoveries

1   What kind of words are the teens using in their speech? How do such words work?

_____

_____

2   Write some common abbreviations you use and what they stand for.

_____

_____

Delving More Deeply

1   What is the cartoonist saying about American teens?

_____

2   The cartoon's caption reads, "PXT. Mom." This means, "Please explain that. Mom." What point is the cartoonist making?

_____

_____

_____

3 Does the cartoonist approve of the teens' language? How do you know?

_____

4 Is this cartoon funny or effective? Why?

_____

Hidden Depths

1 The teens are speaking as if they were using their cell phones to send text messages. In what ways are the text messages superior to speech?

_____

2 What might the teens lose by expressing their thoughts in text messages rather than in speech?

_____

_____

_____

Extend Yourself

- Talk to teens of various ages to find out when and why real teens are using text messages rather than unabbreviated language. Report your findings to the class.

- Collect text messages and their translations to compile a class dictionary.

- Choose a fairy tale whose plot you know, such as the story of Cinderella, and rewrite it in an abbreviated style like text messaging. Have a classmate read and respond to it.

LESSON 24 News Break

Cross-Curriculum Literacy Links: Mathematics; Science; Health; Work, Employment, and Enterprise; Difference and Diversity

Text Type	Explanation, newspaper article
Purpose	To inform, to explain how or why things are as they are, or how things work
Structure	1 A general statement
	2 Series of statements or events in chronological or logical order
	3 Concluding statement
Features	Logical sequence of details or ideas, may use headings, diagrams, and tables

Shuttle to Take Flight Again Soon

Launch of *Discovery* Planned for Summer 2005

A NASA spokesperson reports that a summer 2005 launch window has been scheduled for the shuttle *Discovery*.

NASA's shuttle program has been grounded since the *Columbia* accident in February 2003 as part of NASA's ambitious Return to Flight program. This program attests to NASA's abilities to learn from mistakes and keep them from recurring.

Since the *Columbia* accident, investigators, engineers, and technicians have worked together to determine the cause of the accident and to prevent it from happening again. Investigators determined that *Columbia* was damaged when a block of insulating foam struck and breached a wing, allowing superheated air to enter and weaken the wing during descent. Not only have engineers made changes to prevent such an accident from recurring, but NASA has also developed strategies to inspect and repair, if necessary, the shuttle in orbit and to keep the crew safe till a rescue mission can be launched if the shuttle is damaged and cannot risk descent and reentry.

Discovery's mission, STS-114, will test new equipment, including the redesigned External Fuel Tank. The crew will practice new procedures and carry spare parts and supplies to the International Space Station. The crews of the shuttle and the ISS will cooperate in a series of three space walks to repair the station's altitude controls and gyroscopes.

First priority for the crew, however, will be to test the new in-flight inspection and repair capacities of the shuttle. The crew will use cameras attached to booms to examine the shuttle's wings and insulation tiles.

Mission commander Col. Eileen Collins leads a crew of six. "I have a very high confidence in flying the orbiters," she told reporters, "very high confidence in the people, in the program." As they train for the mission, Collins says, the crew never forgets the work of the *Columbia* astronauts: "It's time to take what they lived for and what they believed in" and carry NASA's flight program forward. Sometime in May or June, that's what Collins and the *Discovery* crew will do.

On the Surface

1 Of what event does the article inform readers?

_____

2 How long (according to the article) has it been since the last shuttle mission?

_____

3 What kind of work have shuttle engineers and technicians been doing since the last launch?

_____

4 Who will command STS-114? How large is the crew?

_____

5 For what two reasons is the shuttle going to dock with the ISS?

_____

Discoveries

1 Highlight all the technical words used in this article. Use a dictionary to check the meanings of unfamiliar technical words. Share and discuss findings.

2 Check an almanac or look online to find out what NASA stands for.

_____

3 The letters NASA form an acronym. What is an acronym? List other acronyms you know.

_____

_____

Delving More Deeply

1 Explain the connection between the *Columbia* accident and the mission of STS-114.

_____

_____

2 Why is STS-114 a particularly important mission for NASA? What will happen if the mission is not a success?

_____

_____

_____

3 What is the function of the headline and subhead?

_____

_____

4 What does the writer assume readers already know about NASA and the shuttle program? How do you know?

_____

_____

Hidden Depths

1 Why have Col. Eileen Collins's comments been included in this article?

_____

_____

2 In what kinds of publications would readers likely see this article?

_____

_____

Extend Yourself

• Use the Internet to find out what life has been like on the ISS since NASA had to ground the shuttles. How has NASA handled crew rotation and supply needs?

• Research the first launch of the space shuttle program. What were NASA's plans for the program at the time? Report your findings to the class.

• Find out how the names for the orbiters were chosen. What history do these names reflect? Discuss the human desire to explore even when risks are involved.

LESSON 25 Read Between the Lines

Cross-Curriculum Literacy Links: Science; Health; Work, Employment, and Enterprise; Difference and Diversity

Text Type Report, magazine article

Purpose To analyze or present factual information about a class of things, usually by classifying them and then describing their characters

Structure 1 Opening general definition or classification

2 Sequence of related statements about the topic

3 Concluding statement

Features May be organized into sections and subsections, may use headings, uses formal or technical language, may include references

Diet Myths Busted!

You may think you're one healthy chick, but could you be a victim of the many diet myths that surround us?

Girlfriend magazine separates fact from fiction!

myth 1 carbohydrates are fattening Low carb or no carb diets may be in vogue at the moment, but they are not a healthy solution for weight loss. Carbohydrates are only fattening when you add fat to them — for example, by having a creamy sauce on pasta or a high-fat spread such as peanut butter on toast. Foods like bread, pasta and potatoes are an important source of energy and we need them to stay healthy.

myth 2 skipping breakfast makes you lose weight Ditching your morning meal is not the way to weight loss. Eating breakfast every morning actually speeds up your metabolism, making it easier for you to lose weight and giving you the energy your body needs after a night of fasting. Just make sure you eat a balanced breakfast, by sticking to healthy foods like cereal, toast, fruit and yogurt — and save the pancakes and croissants for special occasions.

myth 3 a fat-free diet is the way to go Totally eliminating fat from your diet can be dangerous, as we all need a small amount of fat every day to help our joints and muscles work smoothly. However, there are healthy fats and unhealthy ones, so beware! Opt

for things like olive oil, raw nuts and avocado, while steering clear of anything greasy or sugar-laden.

myth 4 snacking between meals is a no-no Starving yourself from meal to meal slows down your metabolism and your body's capacity for burning fat. Eating smaller amounts of food more frequently is much better, as it increases your metabolic rate, so you'll burn fat faster and also have loads more energy. It's best to snack on things like fruit, veggies, nuts or yogurt.

myth 5 trying out fad diets is a great way to shed weight New diets appear almost every week. It is true that some of them might make you shed weight quickly, but the results are usually very short-term. Often the eating patterns they recommend are extreme (e.g., you eat nothing but cabbage soup and bananas) and lacking in nutrients, meaning that as soon as you go back to your normal eating, the weight will come straight back on — often with a bit more weight besides! Being healthy is about adopting a lifestyle you can maintain from day to day.

myth 6 drinking water helps you lose weight Water keeps us hydrated, fills us up and is calorie-free — so it's great to drink some daily. But in no way is it a substitute for food. By filling up on water instead of eating, you're getting none of the nutrients your body needs and you will literally be unable to function.

"Diet Myths Busted!" by Danielle de Gail. *Girlfriend*, September 2002, P. 129.

On the Surface

1 Circle the answer. A myth is:

   a a fairy tale   **c** a story explaining natural phenomena

   b fine rain   **d** an unmarried woman

2 How many diet myths are exposed as false here?

_____

3 Name three carbohydrate foods mentioned here.

_____

4 Is skipping breakfast recommended here? Why or why not?

_____

5 Is a fat-free diet safe or sensible? Why or why not?

_____

Discoveries

1 This article is written in an informal yet informative style. Underline the informal language. Share findings.

2 Highlight facts and technical terms used in this text. Share findings.

3 Comment on the way this article has been set out or constructed. Is it effectively communicating ideas? Why or why not?

_____

_____

Delving More Deeply

1 Make a list of healthy snacks and explain when and why they should be eaten.

_____

2 What is a "fad" diet and how do fad diets differ from healthy eating plans? Give examples.

_____

3 Should we drink less water? Justify your answer.

_____

_____

4   Summarize the information provided in this article.

_____

5   What is the target audience for this article? Give evidence to support your answer.

_____

Hidden Depths

1   Why would an article like this be published in a magazine for teenage girls?

_____

_____

2   List and explain at least one other diet-related issue that could have been discussed in this article.

_____

_____

_____

_____

Extend Yourself

- Collect a range of magazines and conduct a survey of types of articles. Report on your results and comment on the focus on food, eating, and weight in various magazines.

- Design and create a pamphlet on healthy eating, or diet myths for teenagers.

- Research and write a magazine article on the topic "Americans focus on dieting while children around the world go hungry."

- Is dieting overemphasized in the American media? Debate the topic.

LESSON 26 # Catch That Plane!

Cross-Curriculum Literacy Links: Mathematics

Text Type   Timetable
Purpose   To display information about time, place, and other relevant information efficiently
Structure   Table format using words and numbers
Features   Abbreviations, technical language

Flight Schedule for Crater County Municipal Airport

On Your Way Commuter Airlines, based at CCMA

Mon. June 6

SATURDAY

Flight #	Departing	ETD	Arriving	ETA	Notices
86	ABIA	6:15 AM	CCMA	7:30 AM	on time
62	CCMA	6:32 AM	D/FW	7:32 AM	weather delay
162	D/FW	6:58 AM	CCMA	7:58 AM	weather delay
137	SAI	7:00 AM	CCMA	8:30 AM	on time
150	CCMA	7:05 AM	HH	-------	cancelled
48*	HH	7:15 AM	CCMA	8:45 AM	on time
136	CCMA	7:48 AM	HH	9:18 AM	on time
113	CCMA	8:20 AM	D/FW	8:20 AM	weather delay
191*	CCMA	4:30 PM	D/FW	5:30 PM	weather delay
102	CCMA	4:35 PM	SAI	6:05 PM	on time
18	HI	4:45 PM	CCMA	6:15 PM	on time
177*	CCMA	5:00 PM	SAI	8:30 PM	on time
274	D/FW	5:17 PM	CCMA	6:17 PM	weather delay
72	D/FW	7:50 PM	CCMA	8:50 PM	weather delay
230	D/FW	9:00 PM	CCMA	10:00 PM	weather delay

* Stand-by seating available

Key:

CCMA	Crater County Municipal Airport
D/FW	Dallas / Ft. Worth International Airport
HH	Houston Hobby Airport
HI	Houston International Airport
SAI	San Antonio International Airport
ABIA	Austin-Bergstrom International Airport

On the Surface

1   How many commuter flights leave or arrive at CCMA on June 6?

_____

2   To which airport does On Your Way Commuter Airlines offer the most flights?

_____

3   To what five cities can commuters take flights on the airline?

_____

4   What is the earliest flight a commuter can take from CCMA to Houston on June 6?

_____

5   What is the latest arrival at CCMA on June 6?

_____

Discoveries

1   Why is flight schedule information formatted in columns?

_____

2   The key provides information about some of the abbreviations on the chart. What do the abbreviations ETD and ETA stand for?

_____

3   Why does the schedule use so many abbreviations?

_____

_____

4   What do you notice about the order of the flights on the schedule?

_____

Delving More Deeply

1   What can you assume about the flights that do not have asterisks (*) by their number?

_____

2   What can you assume about the weather in Dallas/Ft. Worth on June 6?

_____

3 Why are the times of departure and arrival only estimates?

_____

_____

_____

4 What could have caused the cancellation of Flight 150 to Houston Hobby?

_____

_____

5 What is the best course of action for commuters who planned to take Flight 150 to Houston Hobby?

_____

_____

_____

Hidden Depths

1 The flights on this chart last from an hour to an hour and a half; they are all short. What does that tell you about the customers of On Your Way Commuter Airlines?

_____

_____

2 What kind of luggage do you think most of the customers of On Your Way Commuter Airlines carry?

_____

_____

Extend Yourself

- Search the Internet for the flight schedules of major airlines. Discuss with classmates which schedules are easiest to access and read, and why.

- Use flight and train schedules to plan a real or imaginary outing and come up with several different means of getting to and from your destination. Price your alternatives and compare the relative time needed.

- Locate and visit the airport nearest you. Ask an airline representative what first-time flyers need to know, and develop a brochure for first-time flyers.

(LESSON 27) Going Home

Cross-Curriculum Literacy Links: History; Geography; Civics and Citizenship; Difference and Diversity; Multicultural Content

Text Type	Narrative
Purpose	To tell a story
Structure	1 Introduction — who or what, where and when
	2 Complication
	3 Series of events
	4 Resolution
Features	Use of past tense, pronouns (words taking the place of nouns, e.g., *he, she, him, her*)

from "The Other Country"

After two years in Sydney teaching English to Vietnamese migrants in Bankstown, Rupa Gomez felt she had to return to Sri Lanka. The insistent "When are you coming back?" in every letter from her father, her mother and Aunty Mary, from Francis and Srini, from everyone excepting Uncle Anthony, took on the collective force behind a battering ram.

The car stopped before the familiar house in St Mary's Road. Srini, her younger sister, ran to the car and hugged Rupa. Everything was the same: the scent of jasmine in the air, the purple profusion of bougainvilleas, latticed sunlight, a strip of diamond-shaped criss-crossings on the verandah floor; potted maidenhair ferns still lining the steps; the same well-worn cane chairs. Why then did she feel that something — someone was missing?

"Where's Uncle Anthony?" she asked abruptly.

They looked at her distressed, mournful. Her mother said, a quiver in her voice, "He — he's dead." Then added, "It's so nice to have you back."

Rupa had vaguely noticed her mother's black-and-white sari, but hadn't taken in the meaning of that choice of colors in the almost heady pleasure of homecoming. "What — what happened?" she asked, her voice unsteady.

"Heart," said Srini tersely. "The funeral's the day after tomorrow."

With tears streaming down her face, Rupa heard rather than saw Aunty Mary. "Crying! People overseas must expect their relatives to die in their absence."

from "The Other Country" by Chitra Fernando, in *Beyond the Echo: Multicultural Women's Writing*, eds., Sneja Gunew and Jan Mahyuddin. St. Lucia: University of Queensland Press, 1988, St. Lucia, P. 133.

On the Surface

1   What is the name of the main character in this narrative?

_____

2 Where did Rupa come from originally?

_____

3 What work does Rupa do?

_____

4 What relation is Srini to Rupa?

_____

5 What happened to Rupa's uncle Anthony?

_____

Discoveries

1 Highlight descriptive words and phrases that appeal to the senses in this text.

_____

2 Circle and label the introduction and resolution sections of this narrative.

_____

3 List as bullet points the series of events in this narrative.

_____

4 Underline words in the past tense in this text.

_____

Delving More Deeply

1 Why did Rupa return to Sri Lanka?

_____

2 What was Rupa's first reaction on returning to her old home?

_____

3 Which sentence provides the complication in this narrative?

_____

4 What clue had Rupa failed to notice that showed that a change had occurred?

_____

Reading Comprehension Across the Genres 6, SV1419023616

5 How did Rupa feel during this homecoming as the events unfolded? Give evidence.

_____

_____

Hidden Depths

1 Explain the phrase "took on the collective force behind a battering ram."

_____

_____

_____

2 What does Aunty Mary mean by her final comment? What possible motivations could this comment reveal?

_____

_____

_____

Extend Yourself

- Act out the homecoming scene.
- Assign characters to class members and rewrite this narrative together as a series of letters between Rupa and her relatives.
- Continue this narrative with Rupa's reply to Aunty Mary.
- Investigate celebrations and burial customs in different cultures. Create a class wall display of your findings.

NAME _____   DATE _____

Connecting Up

Cross-Curriculum Literacy Links: Science; History; Geography; Health; Work, Employment, and Enterprise; Civics and Citizenship

Text Type	Exposition, Web page
Purpose	To persuade by putting forward an argument or particular point of view
Structure	1 Point of view is stated
	2 Justifications of argument in a logical order
	3 Summing up of argument
Features	Facts and figures, logical reasoning, examples, persuasive or emotive language

Rainforest Action Network (RAN) Web Page

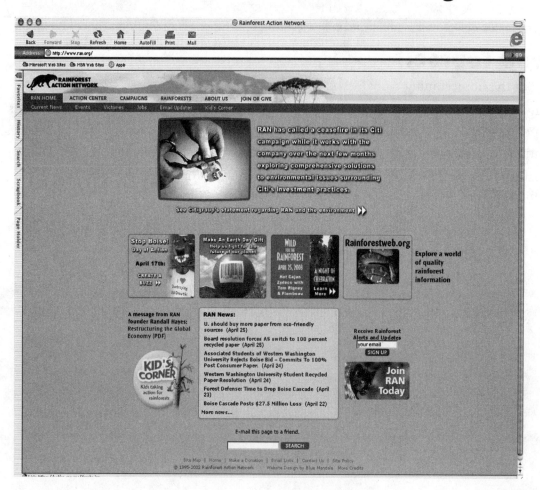

On the Surface

1   Which organization is represented by this Web page?

_____

2   How many major choices are displayed at the top of the Web page?

_____

3   At which address can you "explore a world of quality rainforest information"?

_____

4   Who is the founder of RAN?

_____

5   What suggestion is made at the bottom of the Web page? Why?

_____

_____

Discoveries

1   List all the technical terms used in this text.

_____

2   In groups, select two of these technical terms and discuss how they have been created from existing English words.

3   Combine your class findings on a mind map for display near your school computers.

_____

Delving More Deeply

1   How can you find out ways to save the rainforest using this Web page?

_____

2   Where could you obtain statistics about rainforests using this page?

_____

3   Why might teachers and students use this Web page?

_____

4   Why are there several photographs on this page?

_____

Hidden Depths

1   In your opinion, would this Web page be easy to use? Provide support for your opinion.

_____

_____

_____

_____

2   If you were asked to improve this Web page, what suggestions would you make?

_____

_____

_____

Extend Yourself

• Discuss, as a class, how you could verify information and claims made on a Web site that is designed to convince you of a particular view.

• Create a class directory of recommended Web sites.

• Using a computer, make up and share crosswords or word searches of technical or rainforest vocabulary.

LESSON ㉙ The Big Screen

Cross-Curriculum Literacy Links: Arts; Drama

Text Type	Timetable, cinema program
Purpose	To display information efficiently
Structure	Tabular format of words and numbers
Features	Abbreviations, technical language

Cityside Cinemas
Movie times for December 5th through December 11th

THE PROTECTOR IV (PG)
THU–WED 11:45, 1:00, 2:00, 3:00, 4:15, 5:15, 6:15,
7:30, 8:30, 9:30PM
FRI-SAT 10:45PM

HAPPY FAMILIES (G)
10:00, 12:00, 2:15, 4:35, 6:35, 8:35PM
FRI–SUN 9:30PM

DANCE THE NIGHT AWAY (PG13)
11:10, 1:10, 3:05, 5:05PM
FRI–SUN 7:10PM

SECRET SOCIETY (R)
11:00, 1:30, 4:30, 7:00, 9:45PM

THE MENTOR (G)
3:45PM

LOST CAUSE (R)
10:10, 12:40, 5:20, 9:40PM
FRI–SAT 11:45PM

HIGHWAY HAZE (PG13)
11:50, 3:15, 7:40, 9:50PM

ANNA'S QUEST (PG13)
9:50, 12:00, 2:10, 4:20, 6:30PM

CRUSHED (PG13)
10:00, 12:10, 2:30, 4:40, 6:50, 9:00PM

SHIPWRECKED (PG)
9:55, 1:40, 6:00, 8:00, 9:50PM

www.cityside-cinemas.com
Movie times are subject to change without notice.

On the Surface

1 What is the name of the cinema complex in this text?

_____

2 When are these session times current?

_____

3 How many different films or movies are showing? _____

4 What do the ratings G, PG, PG13, and R mean?

_____

_____

_____

5 How many of these films are suitable for small children and how can you tell?

_____

Discoveries

1 This cinema program is a guide only. It says: "Movie times are subject to change without notice." Discuss why movie times may change suddenly.

2 In groups, think of a fair way to decide what film a group of friends will see.

_____

Delving More Deeply

1 Which films showing at Cityside have titles that indicate their content or theme?

_____

_____

2 Which film appears to be most popular from this program? How can you tell?

_____

3 Which films showing at Cityside are suitable for adults only? Why would this be so?

_____

_____

4 What might *Crushed* be about? Come up with as many possibilities as you can.

_____

Hidden Depths

1   Which films could a group of friends, aged about eleven, see somewhere between 6 and 8 P.M. on Friday 6 December at Cityside Cinemas?

_____

2   Are film ratings necessary, or should customers be unrestricted in their viewing? State your opinion with supporting evidence.

_____

_____

_____

Extend Yourself

• Plan a group or class movie night.

• Write a real film review of your favorite movie.

• Write an imaginary film review of one of the movies showing at Cityside Cinemas.

LESSON 30 Movie Review

Cross-Curriculum Literacy Link: Drama

Text Type	Film review
Structure	Review
	1 Context — background information on the text
	2 Description of the text (including characters and plot)
	3 Concluding statement (judgment, opinion, or recommendation)
Features	Language may be formal or informal depending on purpose and audience, may include examples

DVD Release

The Incredibles

(Approx. 115 mins) PG, Review

by Harley Michaels

2004's Oscar-winning full-length animated feature, *The Incredibles*, is finally out on DVD (and video cassette). This two-disc set from Pixar offers not only a great movie but also a long list of great bonus features.

The movie, written and directed by Brad Bird, who also provides voice talent for the unflappable fashion designer Edna Mode, features a family of superheroes trying to get by in a world that won't let them use their powers. Pixar has already proved, in movies such as *Toy Story* and *Finding Nemo*, its story-telling gifts. The writing team for *The Incredibles* has done it again with the story of super-good versus super-evil.

Disc two contains the charming and wise animated short "Boundin'" that ran before the movie in theaters. Also, "Jack-Jack Attack," a never-before-seen short, explains babysitter Kari's frantic phone calls, and viewers learn that Jack-Jack has super powers after all.

Other features include bloopers and outtakes, filmmakers' comments and a "making of" feature, deleted scenes, and top secret files on all the supers. This two-disc collector's edition is worth its price and is sure to delight viewers of all ages.

On the Surface

1 How long does the film run?

_____

2 What is the film's classification?

_____

3 Who is the director?

_____

4 Who wrote the screenplay?

_____

5 What is the conflict of the film's story?

_____

Discoveries

1 What does Brad Bird do for the film in addition to writing and directing it?

_____

2 The reviewer used the following words to reflect his positive reaction to the film. On a separate piece of paper, rewrite the review for a younger audience, using simpler versions of the words listed below.
— *animated*: rendered in cartoon style, by drawing or in computer graphics
— *voice talent*: the actor who provides the voice for an animated character
— *charming*: appealing and magnetic in personality
— *gifts*: talents, abilities
— *wise*: containing sound teachings
— *frantic*: panicky and hurried
— *bloopers*: mistakes
— *outtakes*: scenes that had to be filmed again or that were cut from the final version
— *deleted*: cut, thrown out

Delving More Deeply

1   Who is the author of this review?

_____

2   How is this film like other films from Pixar's studio?

_____

3   Which features on the two-disc set would most interest someone who wants to make films someday?

_____

4   According to the reviewer, which feature on disc two will teach as well as entertain?

_____

5   What part of the story will be entirely new to viewers who have only seen the movie in the theater?

_____

_____

Hidden Depths

1   Reviews of a film are different from book reviews. What does a film reviewer have to consider that a book reviewer does not?

_____

_____

2   Could this review persuade you to buy the two-disc collector's edition of *The Incredibles?* Why or why not?

_____

_____

Extend Yourself

*   With your parents' permission, view *The Incredibles* (or another animated movie) and write your own review.
*   View "Boundin'" and write a short essay in which you discuss its teaching and whether you agree or disagree with it.
*   Why do you think *The Incredibles* film has been given a PG rating?

LESSON 31 Talk to the Animals

Cross-Curriculum Literacy Link: Drama

Text Type Account

Purpose To reconstruct past experiences by telling events in the order in which they occurred

Structure 1 Introduction— background information about who, where, and when

2 Series of events in chronological order

3 A personal comment

Features Past tense, action verbs, descriptive language, may include quotes

Harriet's Practice

Harriet: Good morning, Buddy. Thank you for joining us.

Buddy: Woof! Do you think I could have one of those biscuits on the plate? Please? Please? I'll sit nicely and everything.

Harriet: OK. Just one.

Buddy: Yeah! Oh boy. [Scoff] Well, that's over.

Harriet: Well Buddy, today's topic is homelessness. What's your story?

Buddy: Well, when I was one month old, I was taken to live in a home. It wasn't very nice: concrete floors, wire cages, and no carpet or TV. One day one of the visitors picked me up and took me home with him. I was so pleased, as he seemed like such a nice man. He had a gentle voice and smiled a lot.

My new home had a TV! So I climbed straight up on the couch. You have to establish your position, you know. The man had other ideas, though. I was soon pushed onto the floor.

Things worked out well. Although I have to admit I got in a bit of trouble.

The man got particularly annoyed when I dug up the plants to put my bone away. What was I to do? I couldn't just leave it out! He tried to teach me to fetch, but I simply don't see the point of bringing the stick back. He just throws it away again! So I hold onto it and he has to chase me while I protect it. I spend a lot of time waiting for him to decide when to go to the park. I try to tell him, but quite often he ignores me. I even take the leash and dump it at his feet.

Then one day I was just hanging around the back yard, as usual. I was so bored. I decided to escape through the back fence. I had a lovely day at the park, marking all the trees and running around. But on my way back to the house I got terribly lost. It was the beginning of the worst week of my life. I managed to find some food from scavenging in garbage bins, but it was not enough. I would spend all day just looking for something to eat. I didn't have much fun.

I was eventually picked up and taken back to the home I lived in when I was young. I was there for a few days before the man came to get me. He looked so relieved to see me.

I have learned my lesson now. I have to wait for the man to go to the park. There is one thing that's changed though — I now can watch TV on the couch!

Harriet: Well, that sounds like a difficult time in your life. Thank you for sharing that with us.

Buddy: That's all right. Can I have another biscuit?

On the Surface

1   What is the name of the program?

_____

2   How old was Buddy when he was taken to the home?

_____

3   What does Harriet have on a plate?

_____

4   Why did Buddy break out of the back yard?

_____

5   What did he spend all day doing when he was lost?

_____

Discoveries

1   How does the interviewer begin the interview?

_____

2   How does Harriet end the interview?

_____

3   How do interviewers on television or radio usually begin and end their interviews?

_____

_____

_____

Delving More Deeply

1   What sort of "home" was Buddy taken to?

_____

2   How does Buddy tell his owner he wants to go to the park?

_____

3   Why do you think the man is so relieved when he sees Buddy?

_____

4   What are Buddy's main priorities in life?

_____

5   Why do you think the man now lets Buddy sit on the couch?

_____

_____

Hidden Depths

1   If you have a pet, or have had a pet, write about the funny things they do. How do they communicate with you? Share your experiences with a partner.

_____

_____

2   Have you ever been lost yourself? Explain what happened and how you felt.

_____

_____

Extend Yourself

- Find out about animal shelters in your area. How are they run? How are they funded? What happens to the dogs? Write a short report on your findings.

- Write up your own interview with one of your pets. Imagine that your pet can talk. What would the pet say about you?

- Watch the Dr. Dolittle films. Write a film review describing some of the animals featured.

- Some people have very unusual pets. Do you know anyone with such pets? Why do they like them?

- Is there a particular pet you would like to have? Explain why.

LESSON 32 Signing Up

Cross-Curriculum Literacy Links: Health; Arts; Work, Employment, and Enterprise

Text Type	Form
Purpose	To record information
Structure	Highly structured, logical format with formalized questions and answers
Features	May include abbreviations, technical or legal language, visual information, a range of fonts

Cityside Tennis Club Membership Application Form

Cityside Tennis Club — Application for Membership

Name: _____

Address: _____

Phone (h): _____ Phone (cell): _____

Phone (w): _____ E-mail: _____

Date of Birth: _____

I, _____, wish to apply for junior/adult/family membership at the Cityside Tennis Club. I agree to abide by the rules of the club as laid out in the "Rules for Members," which I have read and understood. I understand that if I fail to maintain financial membership or by contravening the "Rules for Members," I will no longer be accorded the rights and privileges of membership.

Signed: _____

Date: _____

Annual membership fees:	Junior (<16 yrs)	$ 80
	Adult	$120
	Family	$150
Cityside Tennis Club Hours:	Mon–Fri	8 A.M.–10 P.M.
	Sat	8 A.M.–6 P.M.
	Sun	8 A.M.–2 P.M.

Membership approved

Signed: _____ (Secretary) Date: _____

On the Surface

1   What is this form?

_____

2   Why are three phone numbers required?

_____

3   Name the types of membership available.

_____

4   Why is date of birth necessary on this form?

_____

5   How much does a family membership cost?

_____

Discoveries

1   Highlight official or formal language used in the form.

_____

2   Circle all the places information must be added to the form.

_____

3   As a class, brainstorm the types of forms encountered in daily life.

4   Organize your brainstormed responses using a graphic organizer such as a mind map or Venn diagram. Share and discuss.

Delving More Deeply

1   What must all members of this club agree to do?

_____

2   What might some of the "Rules for Members" be?

_____

_____

3   Explain two ways a member can lose the "rights and privileges" of membership.

_____

4 How many hours each week is the Cityside Tennis Club open to members?

_____

5 What are some advantages and disadvantages of membership in a sports club?

_____

Hidden Depths

1 Would it be better for two siblings to join as junior members or as a family? Why?

_____

2 Why do you think the club would be open at different hours on different days of the week?

_____

_____

Extend Yourself

- With a partner, write your own version of the "Rules for Members" mentioned in the text. Carefully consider the purpose and likely membership of the club.

- As a class, collect as many forms as possible. Discuss similarities and differences and the factors that make a form user-friendly.

- Redesign this form to make it more appealing and user-friendly for junior members.

- Investigate membership fees for various sports clubs and record them in a spreadsheet. Include the benefits that each club offers (or does not offer). Write a paragraph discussing your findings.

www.harcourtschoolsupply.com   **104**   **Lesson 32**
Reading Comprehension Across the Genres 6, SV1419023616

LESSON (33) Not Happy!

Cross-Curriculum Literacy Links: Health; Arts; Work, Employment, and Enterprise; Civics and Citizenship

Text Type	Letter
Purpose	To communicate information, experiences, or ideas (formally or informally) to a reader who is not present
Structure	1 Address and date
	2 Greeting or salutation
	3 Series of events or issues in paragraphs
	4 Closing and signature
Features	Set layout, informal or formal language depending on purpose and audience, varied sentences

Letter of Complaint

Principal Stern
Cityside Middle School
19 Hillview Avenue
Riverton, IL 12987

12/03/2004

Dear Ms. Stern:

My daughter Kim began sixth grade at Cityside Middle School this year. While I am generally pleased with Kim's experience at the school to date, the issue of the range of food offered in the school cafeteria is a source of concern.

Many of Kim's friends use the cafeteria as their main source of nutrition during the school day. However, the list of menu items sent home at the beginning of the school year indicates that much of the menu is made up of high-fat, high-calorie, and highly processed foods. Fresh sandwiches, salads, fruit, yogurt, and fruit juice are either unavailable or in very short supply.

Consequently, I do not permit Kim to use the school cafeteria. However, this has become an unnecessary source of conflict in our home and is an inconvenience, since I am a single mother and work long hours.

Although I am fully aware the cafeteria operates as a business, I believe it is the school's responsibility to present healthy food choices to students and to promote long-term, healthy lifestyle choices. Cafeterias at many other schools operate successfully on this basis.

Please regard this letter as a formal complaint. Furthermore, it is my intention to raise this matter publicly at the next PTA meeting and to pursue a change in the policy and menu of the cafeteria.

Thank you for your consideration of this matter.

Yours sincerely,

Katy O'Day

On the Surface

1   Who wrote this letter?

_____

2   To whom is this letter addressed?

_____

3   What is Ms. O'Day complaining about?

_____

4   Is Kim allowed to buy food from the cafeteria? Why not?

_____

5   What is Ms. O'Day planning to do about this concern?

_____

Discoveries

1   Read this letter aloud with expression. Then describe the tone of the letter.

_____

2   Underline the words and phrases that help create the tone of this letter. Share and discuss.

3   Why has Ms. O'Day written this letter instead of phoning the principal?

_____

_____

Delving More Deeply

1   Do Kim and Ms. O'Day agree about this issue? How do we know?

_____

2   Would Ms. O'Day let Kim use the cafeteria if the menu were changed? Why?

_____

3   What is Ms. O'Day's opinion of Cityside Middle School in general?

_____

_____

4 What foods does Ms. O'Day think should be sold in the cafeteria?

_____

_____

5 What does the phrase "I am fully aware the cafeteria operates as a business" suggest?

_____

_____

Hidden Depths

1 How do you think Kim would feel about Ms. O'Day's letter?

_____

2 How do you think the principal would (a) feel about and (b) react to Ms. O'Day's letter?

_____

Extend Yourself

- Role-play this complaint as a phone call rather than a letter.
- Role-play arguments between Ms. O'Day and Kim about the cafeteria and the writing of this letter.
- Write a reply to Ms. O'Day from the principal.
- Debate the topic that school cafeterias have a responsibility for children's health.
- Investigate your own school cafeteria's menu. Divide the foods available into healthy and unhealthy choices.

NAME _____   DATE _____

What's for Lunch?

Cross-Curriculum Literacy Links: Science; Health; Arts; Work, Employment, and Enterprise; Civics and Citizenship

Text Type	Menu
Purpose	To display available food choices
Structure	Varied but logical groupings of dishes
Features	Technical language relating to ingredients and food preparation

Proposed School Cafeteria Menu

After discussion, the PTA, Students Representative Council, and cafeteria management of Cityside Middle School propose the following new Cityside Middle School cafeteria menu. The new menu is being published in the school newsletter for comment by members of the school community.

SANDWICHES	MUFFINS — low-fat, high-fiber
(Rolls or pita bread available as alternatives)	Apple & cinnamon
Tuna salad	Banana
Chicken salad	Blueberry
Cheese	Apricot & almond
Cheese & lettuce	Carrot
Egg & lettuce	Raisin
Ham	**HOT FOOD**
Turkey	Soft taco
Chicken	Sausage wrap
Roast beef	Hot dog
Peanut butter	Noodles
Avocado and sprouts	Vegetable soup
FRUIT	**SWEETS & SNACKS**
Apple	Fruit juice snacks
Orange	Jelly beans
Banana	Chocolate-covered nuts
Fruit salad	Potato chips
YOGURT	Granola bars
Low-fat fruit	**DRINKS**
Low-fat frozen	Milk / juices / mineral water

On the Surface

1 List the categories of food available on this menu.

_____

2 How many varieties of sandwiches are available? _____

3 Which categories of food on the menu contain fruit?

_____

4 Which hot foods on the menu could a vegetarian eat?

_____

5 Which foods on the menu contain vegetables?

_____

_____

Discoveries

1 In groups, use this menu to create a computer form for the cafeteria staff to use when ordering supplies each week. Share and discuss.

2 In pairs, create a comment form to be included in the newsletter so that the school community can respond to the proposal. Which form — Yes/No, multiple-choice, or open-ended — is more efficient and effective? Share and discuss.

Delving More Deeply

1 Why would two forms of yogurt be offered on the menu?

_____

_____

2 Are the muffins a healthy alternative to cakes and cookies? Why?

_____

3 Which foods should someone allergic to nuts avoid on this menu?

_____

_____

4 Why have granola bars been included in the sweets and snacks category?

_____

5 What popular group of drinks has been left off the menu? Why?

_____

_____

Hidden Depths

1 Which categories on the menu contain the least healthy foods, and why do you think they have
   been included?

_____

_____

2 In groups, create a variety of lunch orders using this menu; then rank the menus on nutritional
   value (using criteria such as amounts of calories, fat, sugar, carbohydrates, protein, and fiber).
   How successful is the menu at promoting healthy eating habits? Share and discuss.

Extend Yourself

- Role-play various reactions to the new menu between students and students, students and parents,
  and parents and the cafeteria staff.

- Reformat the menu to make it more logical.

- Discuss what could be added to the menu to make it visually appealing.

- Carry out a class survey on what should and should not be included in school cafeteria menus.

- Make a class collection of menus with a food critics' section on a bulletin board in your
  classroom.

LESSON 35 # Cravings

Cross-Curriculum Literacy Links: Science; Health; Difference and Diversity

Text Type	Procedure
Purpose	To give instructions or show how something is accomplished through a series of steps
Structure	1 Opening statement of goal or aim
	2 Materials required listed in order of use
	3 Series of steps listed in chronological order
Features	Logical sequence of steps, may use technical language and diagrams

BLT Recipe

Make delicious bacon, lettuce, and tomato toasted sandwiches for a great lunch or light main meal.

Ingredients:	4 slices bacon
	4 slices thick bread, toasted
	2 large lettuce leaves
	1 small ripe tomato
	2 level tablespoons mayonnaise
Preparation time:	15 minutes
Cooking time:	5 minutes
Serves:	2

Method:

1 Cook the bacon until crisp and brown in a frying pan or the microwave.

2 Toast the bread and spread with the mayonnaise.

3 Slice the tomato.

4 Tear the lettuce into small segments.

5 Place a slice of toast onto each of two plates.

6 Place the lettuce, tomato, and 2 slices of bacon on top of the toast and top with the remaining slices of toast.

7 Cut the sandwiches into triangles and serve immediately.

On the Surface

1   What is this a recipe for?

_____

2   How many ingredients will you need to make this recipe?

_____

3   How long does it take to make this recipe?

_____

4   How many people will this recipe serve?

_____

5   How many steps does the recipe involve?

_____

Discoveries

1   Is the order of the steps in this recipe important and/or logical? In a group, discuss alternative ordering of the steps.

_____

2   Why is the language in each step impersonal? Rewrite each step as you would actually explain it to a friend.

_____

3   Underline the verbs or action words in the steps. Where do they occur in the sentences? Is this placement effective? Is it common in how-to texts?

_____

Delving More Deeply

1   When might you eat a BLT?

_____

2   Why is the cooking time shorter than the preparation time?

_____

_____

_____

3 How many slices of bread would you need to make four servings of this recipe?

_____

4 Is it necessary to cut the sandwiches into triangles? Why is it recommended?

_____

_____

Hidden Depths

1 Is this recipe safe for sixth-graders to prepare? What steps might present risks, and how can cooks avoid these risks?

_____

2 This recipe is reasonably nutritious but could be improved. Suggest ways to make a healthier BLT.

_____

Extend Yourself

- Make a class recipe book by compiling favorite recipes.
- Choose a recipe and rewrite it, making it healthier.
- Organize and hold a class lunch to share favorite recipes.
- Invent as many different sorts of sandwiches as you can and create a menu for a sandwich shop.
- Investigate recent recipes published in magazines. What current cooking and eating trends are revealed in these publications?

Main Idea Web

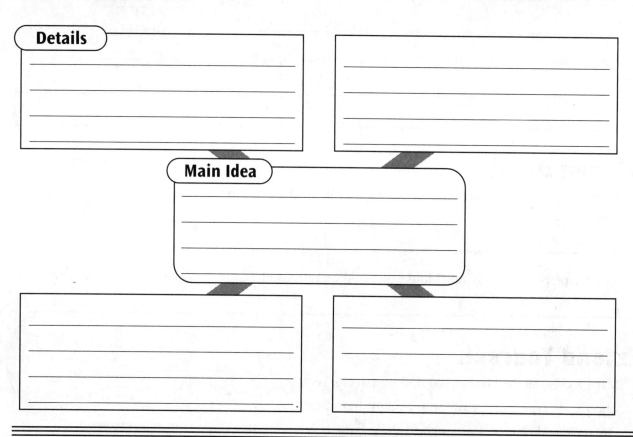

Story Map

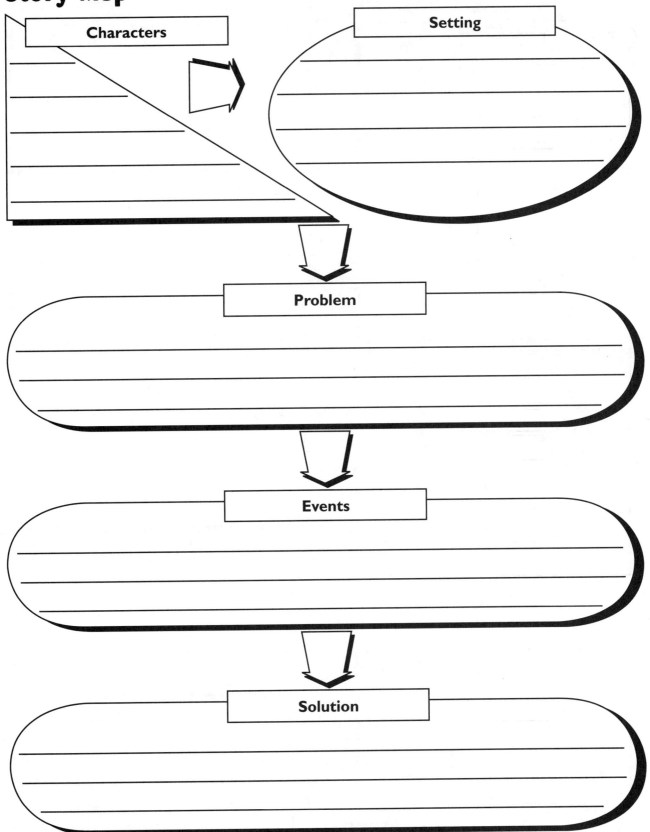

Characters

Setting

Problem

Events

Solution

Cause and Effect Charts

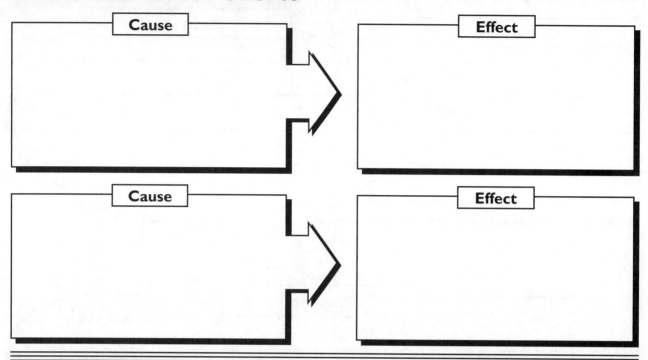

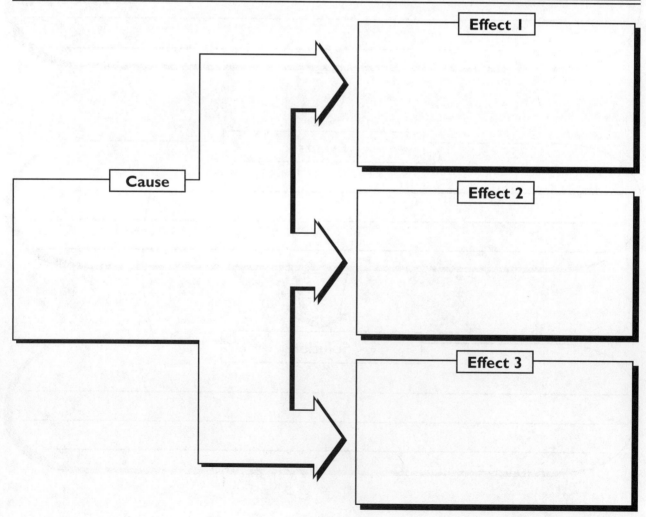

NAME _____   DATE _____

Venn Diagram

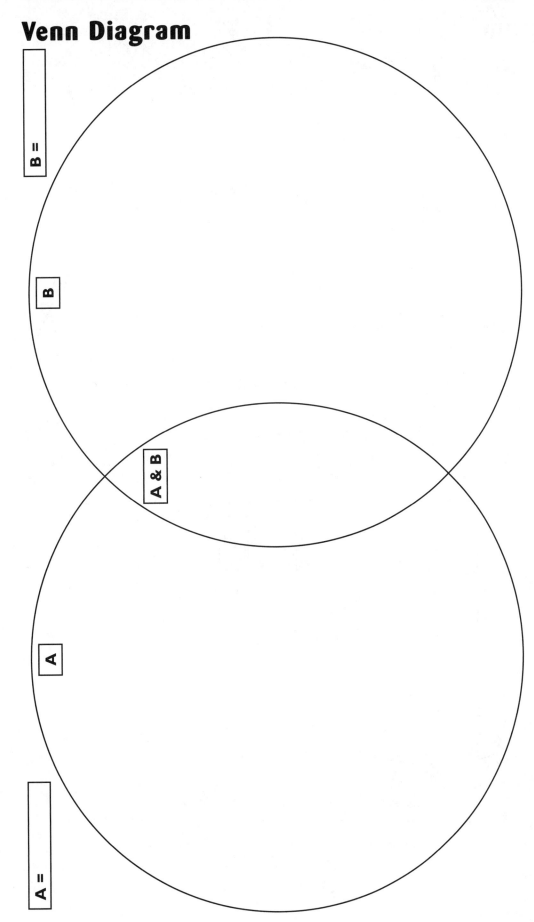

B =

B

A & B

A

A =

Venn Diagram

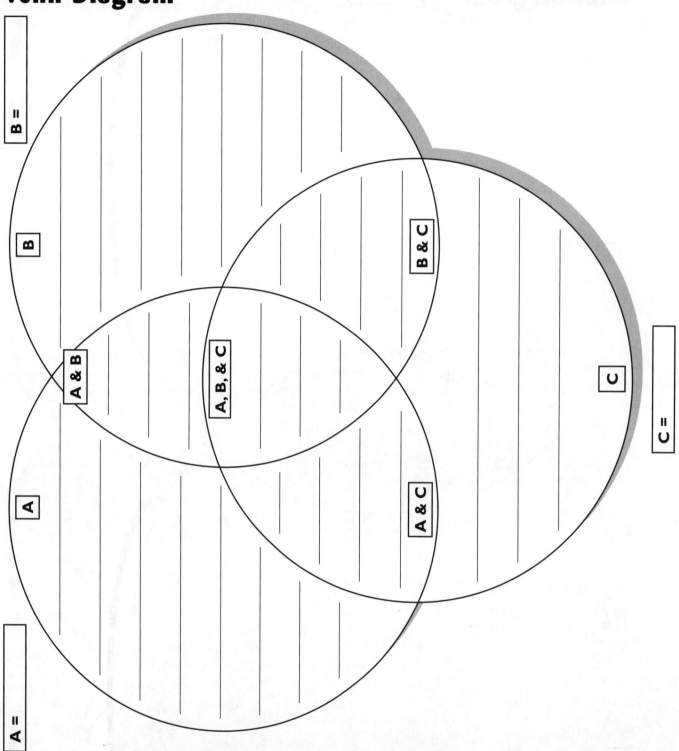

B =

B

B & C

A & B

A, B, & C

C

A

A & C

A =

Graphic Organizers: Venn Diagram (3)
Reading Comprehension Across the Genres 6, SV1419023616

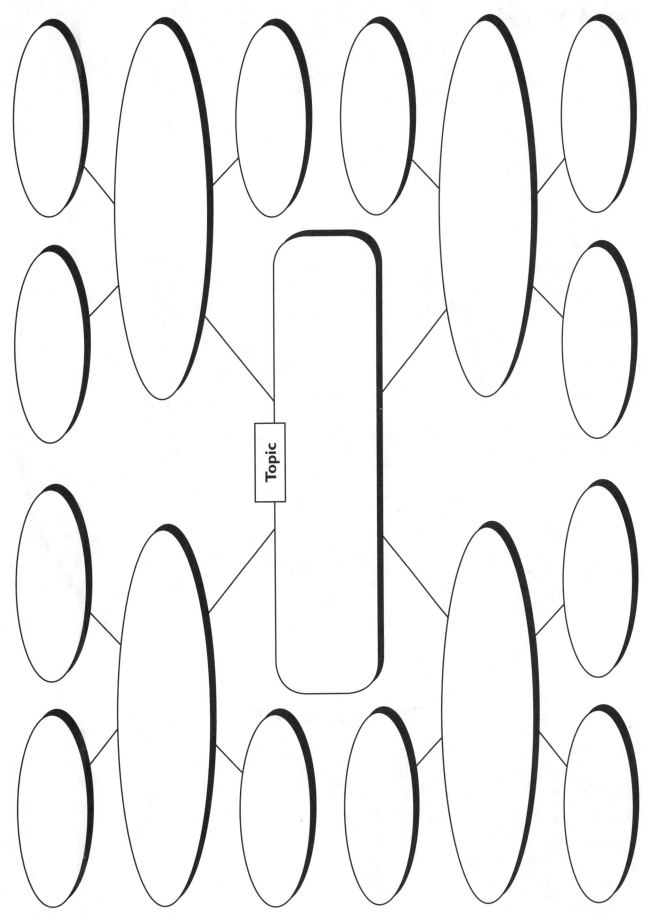

Topic

Graphic Organizers: Word Web
Reading Comprehension Across the Genres 6, SV1419023616

Word Wheel

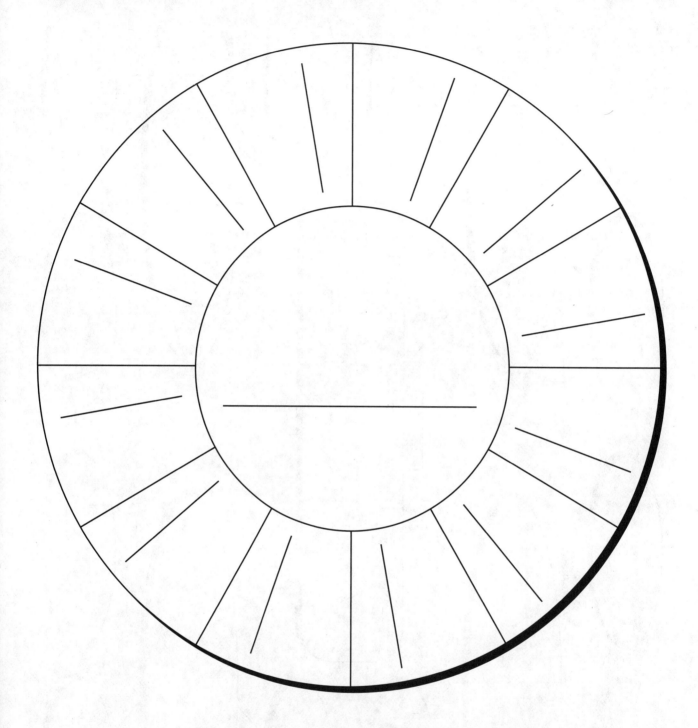

Reading Comprehension Across the Genres, Grade 6

Answer Key

Lesson 1, pages 9–11
On the Surface
1. the policeman and the waiting man
2. a scar by his eye and a large diamond in his scarf pin
3. twenty years
4. late at night, in a doorway on an empty street, chilly wet weather
5. an appointment he made twenty years ago

Discoveries
1. **a.** complicated
   b. peaceful
   c. sturdy, strong
   d. strut, proud gait
2. **a.** empty, vacated
   b. street
   c. area
3. Responses will vary.

Delving More Deeply
1. The police officer is confident, good at his job, polite. The waiting man is optimistic that his friend will appear.
2. He does not want to be suspected of illegal behavior.
3. He liked New York too much to leave.
4. Perhaps he has seen some trouble or violence, but he has been successful despite it.
5. He is not worried in the dark; he is watchful; he checks doors; he approaches the man carefully but without fear; he knows his beat, or neighborhood, well.

Hidden Depths
1. People couldn't travel fast then. The man probably had to travel by train for days. He had to be determined to spend the time and money to keep the appointment.
2. Responses will vary. Share and discuss.

Lesson 2, pages 12–14
On the Surface
1. August 15th at noon
2. five
3. from gales, to moderate breezes, to clear, to misty
4. 5 miles
5. much apprehension

Discoveries
1. **a.** concern, fear
   b. strong wind
   c. six feet of water
   d. high land jutting into the sea
2. Time, Latitude South, Longitude East, Observations
3. **a.** south
   b. east

Delving More Deeply
1. Responses will vary.
2. the number of seabirds and the fact that they can see land
3. to test the depth of the water
4. No. The vegetation is unfamiliar to them.
5. Yes. Smoke is seen from fires on land.

Hidden Depths
1. Responses will vary but should include sailors' apprehension.
2. Responses will vary.

Lesson 3, pages 15–17
On the Surface
1. Camp Scorcher
2. Monday until Friday, 5 days
3. bus
4. burgers, BBQ, chicken & salad, spaghetti

5. night woods walk, archery, raft building, low ropes, high ropes, swimming, canoeing, horseback riding, challenge course, skits

Discoveries
1. **a.** hot day
   b. short play
2. Answers will vary.
3. On Monday, 9 A.M., took ages, 20 minutes late, 2 P.M., after we unpacked, then, at night, on Wednesday, most of the afternoon, after dinner, Thursday, on Friday
4. ages, millions of trees, scorcher
5. burgers
   Tuesday; archery, raft building, low ropes, stories, campfire; BBQ
   Wednesday; high ropes, canoeing, horseback riding, swimming, skit planning; chicken and salad
   Thursday; challenge course, "Limelight Night"; spaghetti
   Friday; clean up, pack up, awards

Delving More Deeply
1. Responses will vary.
2. Scorcher is slang for very hot weather and the camp was very hot.
3. Responses will vary. The students had to provide entertainment for each other and work cooperatively.
4. Yes. Concerned about coming second in challenge course; pleased to win "Limelight"; mentions certificate of participation and chocolate bar
5. Responses will vary; tired because it had been a busy and social week with little quiet time, sad because it had been a great week together.

Hidden Depths
1. e
2. Responses will vary.

Lesson 4, pages 18–20
On the Surface
1. Ms. Francine Price, Grade 6 Coordinator
2. parents or guardians of Grade 6 students
3. trained camp personnel and school staff
4. a student, Sam
5. Camp Scorcher

Discoveries
1. **a.** staff
   b. responsible adult
2. Share and discuss.
3. Responses will vary.

Delving More Deeply
1. d
2. three
3. No, it's part of the school's program.
4. Yes, Sam thought he would hate camp.
5. Yes, he mentions them in phrases such as ". . . do we ever," "our skit."

Hidden Depths
1. First is formal; second is informal. Differences: known or unknown audience, business or social purpose, authoritative language and correct grammatical structures versus casual language and speech-like phrasing.
2. No, Sam will be home again too soon.

Lesson 5, pages 21–23
On the Surface
1. muscular organ maintaining circulation of blood
2. eleven
3. Students should draw traditional heart shape.
4. red
5. heart

Discoveries
1. Responses will vary.
2. Responses will vary. Share and discuss.

Delving More Deeply
1. Responses will vary.
2. Responses will vary.
3. They would try to stop smoking; maybe they would get help from a doctor.
4. It is an example of figurative language; it shows we regard the hurt as very serious because the heart is so important.
5. c

Hidden Depths
1. **a.** false
   b. true
   c. true
   d. false
2. Responses will vary.

Lesson 6, pages 24–26
On the Surface
1. Libby, Sarah, and Rebecca
2. They are in a hair salon, where Libby is working on Sarah's hair and Rebecca is sweeping.
3. She is worried about a birthday celebration.
4. sweeping the salon floor
5. to throw a surprise party and invite all her friends

Discoveries
1. Lib, for Libby, and Becca, for Rebecca; they are close enough friends to use nicknames.
2. She means that Sarah is nervous and won't hold still, like ants, which are rarely still.

Delving More Deeply
1. He said he didn't want a party, but he has demonstrated that he doesn't always mean what he says.
2. The ellipses (. . .) and dashes show that her thoughts are unfinished and unsure.
3. Responses will vary. Share and discuss. The two are friends, but some hairdressers use pet names with all clients.
4. **a.** confidence; an in-charge, can-do attitude
   b. worried about Jake, unsure, looking for help
   c. worried about being left out, hoping for a party

Hidden Depths
1. Responses will vary. She uses slang, drops final consonants, is very assertive, and gives orders. She sounds like she knows what she wants and gets it, but is still friendly.
2. names of speakers, layout, stage directions in brackets

Lesson 7, pages 27–29
On the Surface
1. physical weathering of rocks
2. Wear safety glasses and follow lab rules.
3. three
4. Number 1 has to be left overnight.
5. So you won't get burned.

Discoveries
1. **a.** test, trial
   b. protection
   c. edge, lip
   d. piece
   e. a kind of sedimentary rock
   f. exterior, face
   g. steps, method
   h. deposit, what is left behind
2. Share and discuss.
3. Students should discuss purpose, impersonal nature of language used, stress structure and features of procedural texts.
4. add diagrams; use "plain English"

Delving More Deeply
1. safety glasses, bottle with screw top lid, water, plastic bag, freezer, shale, pan, sand tray heating source, tongs, Bunsen burner, granite, pan, cold water
2. reezes, ottle, rack

3. The same results would occur for larger rocks, so small samples are used for efficiency, expense, and practical reasons.
4. ce, ater, eat
5. The language is condensed and technical, so diagrams would reinforce understanding.

Hidden Depths
1. geology, the study of Earth's crust; the experiments show how Earth's surface changes
2. Hypotheses will vary.

Lesson 8, pages 30–32
On the Surface
1. weathering and erosion of rocks
2. as unchanging
3. fragments of the rock around its base
4. wind, water, and sun
5. movement of weathered rock

Discoveries
1. e.g.: weathering, erosion, landforms, fragments, weathered, eroded, deposition
2. Teacher to discuss and mark. Share and discuss.

Delving More Deeply
1. Responses will vary.
2. The location determines how much wind, water (ice), and sun the rock is exposed to.
3. The farmland loses topsoil, which is best for growing crops.
4. Yes, because weathering, erosion, and deposition will keep happening.
5. science textbook, geography textbook, natural history magazine, Web site

Hidden Depths
1. Responses will vary. Writer uses personal pronouns we, you, our.
2. Responses will vary. use of photographs or diagrams; layout; font

Lesson 9, pages 33–35
On the Surface
1. Ahla, capital of Mars
2. McKay, Sterling, Ross, about 100 Martians
3. by underground car, 2000 miles, in tunnels
4. Grecian garments, like togas or tunics
5. b

Discoveries
1. **a.** unfamiliar, weird
   b. humbly, respectfully
   c. doorway, entrance
   d. coming from Greek culture
   e. threat
   f. go with
2. Share and discuss responses.

Delving More Deeply
1. It's set in another world and uses aliens as characters.
2. Earth explorers are meeting Martians for the first time.
3. curiosity, calmness, no hostility, welcoming
4. to show goodwill, peace; may be a gesture of superiority; conquistadors; Lewis and Clark and the Native American tribes
5. c, d

Hidden Depths
1. Share and discuss.
2. excited, scared: "hesitated on the threshold . . ."; then relieved: "It's going to be okay."

Lesson 10, pages 36–38
On the Surface
1. to help express ideas clearly in writing and to increase vocabulary
2. explain, clarify, justify, solve
3. verb
4. This indicates they are main entry words and that a full list of associated words follows.
5. colloquial, informal usage

Discoveries
1. Responses will vary. Share and discuss.
2. Responses will vary. Share and discuss.

Delving More Deeply
1. A comment could be, "I agree/disagree because . . ."; illustrating would be based on examples.
2. crime, legal, or police shows
3. crimes, mysteries, investigations by the media, social or emotional problems, medical situations
4. Responses will vary.
5. It means that the product clears the skin of blemishes; sounds scientific and technical, or sounds poetic.

Hidden Depths
1. The reader is inferring information or ideas or meaning that is not directly stated.
2. Justify; its meaning is quite specific and associated largely with legal language.

Lesson 11, pages 39–41
On the Surface
1. *High Score! The Illustrated History of Electronic Games*
2. Rusel Demaria and Johnny L. Wilson
3. Joshua Gliddon
4. It was published in *The Bulletin* magazine.
5. the history of computer games

Discoveries
1. Share and discuss.
2. because they ran on machines that couldn't be programmed for other purposes

Delving More Deeply
1. Yes. It is interesting, nostalgic, and has interesting illustrations.
2. anyone interested in computer games, especially people who were teenagers or young adults in the 1970s
3. nonfiction, history, hobbies and games, science and technology
4. to demonstrate the capabilities of a newly designed minicomputer in the 1960s
5. because the inventors were science fiction fans

Hidden Depths
1. mixed connotations, smart but uncool; now considered cool
2. SpaceWar was the first true computer game and inspired spin-offs. The discussion gives the reader a taste of the sort of information available in the book.

Lesson 12, pages 42–44
On the Surface
1. the scientific study of a culture or civilization by the excavation and description of its remains
2. history, by providing sources of evidence
3. places, objects, tools, trash
4. buildings, ruins, campsites, caves, ships, trash dumps, fields, farms, monuments
5. books, journals, maps, photographs, notes, museum exhibits, Web sites

Discoveries
1. **a.** the act of digging up
   b. an object produced by a culture
   c. threw away
2. e.g.: discovering, searching, investigate, digging
3. Greek "archaios" + "-ology" = study of ancient history; responses will vary.

Delving More Deeply
1. d
2. These materials decay faster than pottery and metal and so are not available centuries later.
3. note its location, measure it and record data, store it

4. It's like solving a jigsaw puzzle because it involves putting the available pieces together to form a picture of the past.
5. They try to reconstruct events and lifestyles of the past.

Hidden Depths
1. patience, interest, keen observation, good coordination, attention to detail
2. out of respect for the people of the past (and their modern-day descendants) and their customs and beliefs, particularly with burial sites

Lesson 13, pages 45–47
On the Surface
1. grandfather; "I wish I'd known my grandfather."
2. **a.** false
   b. true
   c. false
3. thirty years
4. reciting the works of Charles Dickens publicly at Christmas
5. as "thoughtfully astute," in "plump health," with "coolly analytical" gaze

Discoveries
1. Share and discuss.
2. The author is reflected in the glass surface of the portrait; she is writing and shares a love of language with her grandfather.

Delving More Deeply
1. She "worshipped his memory" and kept his clothes and his portrait.
2. a
3. "It was said [people] wept and laughed, and wept and went home in high spirits."
4. It was of Charles Dickens and was signed, or autographed.
5. He died before she was born or when she was very young.

Hidden Depths
1. Discuss evidence and limits of evidence; portraits show people at their best; legends grow over time.
2. mid to late 19th century

Lesson 14, pages 48–50
On the Surface
1. the south, in the bottom right-hand corner
2. He was a ship's captain.
3. He was a naval surgeon, or doctor.
4. to discover if a strait existed and if Tasmania was an island
5. an open whaleboat

Discoveries
1. Share and discuss.
2. Share and discuss.

Delving More Deeply
1. They shouldn't have been able to escape or survive, so it was unlikely to find them on a small island in an isolated area of the country.
2. The boat and supplies were inadequate.
3. Responses will vary. Share and discuss.
4. They were friends, and Governor Hunter wanted them to finish the task.
5. Bass, with Flinders, was the first to map it and locate it, even though their first attempt failed.

Hidden Depths
1. Discuss: adventurous, curious, patient, determined, etc.
2. exhausted but overjoyed, proud

Lesson 15, pages 51–53
On the Surface
1. Australia
2. Indian Ocean, South Pacific Ocean, Coral Sea, Tasman Sea, Arafura Sea, Timor Sea
3. four
4. The Darling River and the Murray River
5. The Great Dividing Range

Discoveries
1. ⌃⌃⌃ and 〜
2. four times, meaning large or huge

Delving More Deeply
1. Indonesia, East Timor, Papua New Guinea, and the Solomon Islands
2. New Caledonia or Vanuatu
3. French, because it is a French territory
4. Torres Strait
5. The Tasman Sea and Tasmania are named after him.

Hidden Depths
1. desert conditions in the central area, small population, need for water and arable land
2. Our continent is much larger and is linked to South America. Together, North and South America span the globe and have many different climate zones.

Lesson 16, pages 54–56
On the Surface
1. to determine population growth and evaluate general health of populations
2. the number of average births or deaths per 1,000 people in the population
3. Africa
4. Europe
5. approximately 15 deaths per 1000 people in Africa

Discoveries
1. a. one who studies population facts
   b. number of people
   c. show, indicate
2. Discuss: The graph gives a visual representation of the facts that is sometimes easier to understand than text would be.
3. in the newspaper, in science and geography texts, on TV

Delving More Deeply
1. They use birth and death rates to determine population growth and evaluate the general health of the populations they study.
2. Share and discuss.
3. Europe
4. Share and discuss using map; group of islands in the South Pacific including Melanesia, Micronesia, Polynesia, and sometimes Australasia and the Malay Archipelago

Hidden Depths
1. Latin America and Asia; responses will vary.
2. lack of resources leading to shortages of food, water, and energy; increased death rates; and conflicts between nations

Lesson 17, pages 57–59
On the Surface
1. the total number of humans living in an area
2. migration, births, and deaths
3. advances in agriculture, industry, scientific knowledge, medicine, and social organization
4. five-fold, 500%, from 500 million to 2.5 billion
5. control of famine and disease; larger crop harvests

Discoveries
1. a. shape, change
   b. not living
   c. living organism that lives off another living organism
2. a. composition
   b. yield
   c. gradually
   d. inanimate
   e. applied
3. Share and discuss—formal, technical language; authoritative and objective tone.

Delving More Deeply
1. More food and more varieties of food would be available so people would live longer, healthier lives.
2. People are cured of diseases that would once have killed them, so they live longer.

3. There are fewer diseases from dirty water. Better waste disposal means disease isn't spread as easily.
4. about 35–40 years
5. Share and discuss pros and cons.

Hidden Depths
1. Share and discuss.
2. textile machines, transport machines, tractors, etc.

Lesson 18, pages 60–62
On the Surface
1. a family with a father, mother, grandmother, and children
2. stones falling from the mountain, fierce winds, and cold
3. They are gathered around the fire for warmth, light, and company, talking and telling jokes.
4. A strong gust of cold wind rattles the door.
5. A traveler arrives unexpectedly.

Discoveries
1. a. calm, wise
   b. located
   c. severity
   d. joke
   e. expression of sorrow
   f. cheerless, grim
   g. announced
2. gathered, piled, roared, brightened, had, was, sat, found, descended, etc.

Delving More Deeply
1. They are not alarmed but rather happy that someone has come to their home.
2. They had found the secret to happiness in their simple family life.
3. the roaring fire that brightened the room; sober gladness; laughter; image of Happiness, knitting in warmest place; herb, heart's-ease; contrast between cold, wind, and danger outside and warmth and coziness inside
4. Responses will vary. Share and discuss. Perhaps they cannot afford to relocate. Perhaps generations of the family have lived there before them.
5. It is probably a river that flows through the valley, since water flows downhill.

Hidden Depths
1. Responses will vary. Share and discuss. The family lives in an out-of-the-way place where there is little danger from strangers. The family is glad to see a new face.
2. Responses will vary. Share and discuss. He will be cared for and entertained as an honored guest and will come to appreciate the family.

Lesson 19, pages 63–65
On the Surface
1. kitten food
2. El Gatito Kitten Food
3. to help kittens grow up strong and healthy
4. El Gatito
5. phosphorous and calcium in the right ratio

Discoveries
1. Three. The large font at the top draws attention to the main idea of the ad. The cursive font is part of the brand's style. The text font is easy to read.
2. Less effective—all kitten food looks pretty much alike. The picture of the cute kitten is more effective in getting readers to like the product.

Delving More Deeply
1. "The responsibility is yours, the food is El Gatito" suggests that the company and the cat owner are partners in raising the cat.
2. "It's up to you, her caregiver, to see she gets the proper diet. . . ."
3. It may be an attempt to get people to act quickly and buy the product.
4. It provides proteins that are easily digestible.

5. It uses a photo of a really cute kitten; it explains what good nutrition includes; and it compliments cat owners by implying that they are good, responsible people.

Hidden Depths
1. Responses will vary. Teacher to lead discussion.
2. older teenagers and adults who own cats; in a newspaper or magazine that carries articles about pets, in a pet store, in a vet's office

Lesson 20, pages 66–68
On the Surface
1. RAN
2. stabilize climate, preserve wildlife habitat, maintain soil productivity
3. Randy Hayes
4. since 1985
5. RAN convinced Burger King to stop buying beef raised in the rainforests.

Discoveries
1. Share and discuss.
2. Only one side; purpose is to promote this organization and viewpoint.
3. angry, annoyed, afraid; sue RAN, run advertising showing another viewpoint, try to damage reputation of RAN, laugh at RAN, ignore RAN, work with RAN

Delving More Deeply
1. to protect the rainforests and support the rights of their inhabitants
2. education, grassroots organizing, and non-violent direct action
3. a campaign that is carried out by everyday people, not by lawyers or politicians
4. Rainforests are cleared to provide pastures for cheap beef production for some hamburger manufacturers.
5. an organized refusal to do something in order to show disapproval or to assert pressure

Hidden Depths
1. to involve ordinary people, to raise public awareness, to gain media attention, to be effective but not costly, to appeal to young people
2. loss of employment and income for some workers, more expensive products resulting from changes of policy

Lesson 21, pages 69–71
On the Surface
1. Twenty Questions
2. two or more
3. animal, vegetable, mineral, or combined
4. The player is out of the game until the next round.
5. The same player stays "it" and has another turn, choosing a different object.

Discoveries
1. Responses will vary. Share and discuss.
2. Responses will vary. Share and discuss.
3. Responses will vary. Share and discuss.

Delving More Deeply
1. Play the game in reverse.
2. Responses will vary. Share and discuss.
3. the meanings of categories, ability to ask questions, counting, good vocabulary, logical thinking, good imagination, and varied experiences
4. It depends; computer games and TV are more popular than word games; families are smaller and spend less time together than in the past. However, it might be played on car trips and with younger children.
5. inexpensive, easy, can play in car, but could be difficult with mixed ages

Hidden Depths
1. Guessers have to remember answers to questions and use the processes of categorization and elimination.
2. Responses will vary. Share and discuss.

Lesson 22, pages 72–74
On the Surface
1. Responses will vary. Share and discuss.
2. a society that cares most about creating wealth and producing goods
3. plants, animals, minerals, water, air
4. earth, air, and water
5. two

Discoveries
1. a. those who expect bad
   b. those who expect good
   c. answers
   d. opinion
   e. no longer existing
2. in a journal, textbook, magazine; on a Web site
3. formal, objective, balanced, technical; e.g., "solutions," "strict governmental management"

Delving More Deeply
1. Responses will vary. Wealthy, industrialized nations like USA, Britain, and Australia as well as developing nations are concerned with resources.
2. Responses will vary. Share and discuss.
3. One, if correct, will result in bad repercussions for humanity; the other will have a positive outcome.
4. Responses will vary. Share and discuss.
5. Responses will vary. Share and discuss.

Hidden Depths
1. statistics, graphs, maps, case studies
2. examples of problems overcome in the past — diseases, transportation, space exploration, genetic engineering

Lesson 23, pages 75–77
On the Surface
1. It's not English; it looks like a bunch of abbreviations.
2. sitting and chatting
3. Responses will vary. The abbreviations mean "What's up this weekend?"
4. Responses will vary. One teen indicates that she will go to a concert with her boyfriend and asks "You, too?" The other agrees with the plan and says she must leave.
5. this, concert, now, Mom

Discoveries
1. They are using abbreviations, in which only part of a word is given and the rest must be inferred.
2. Responses will vary. Examples: USA for United States of America, Dr. for doctor

Delving More Deeply
1. They have a language all their own and enjoy using it.
2. The abbreviated language that the teens use excludes adults from their conversation.
3. Responses will vary. Share and discuss.
4. Responses will vary. Share and discuss.

Hidden Depths
1. They take less room and time and express a lot in a little bit of language.
2. Responses will vary; e.g., they might lose figurative speech, the chance to explain themselves thoroughly, ways to express deep or personal thoughts and feelings.

Lesson 24, pages 78–80
On the Surface
1. an upcoming launch of NASA shuttle *Discovery*
2. over two years
3. working on ways to detect and repair shuttle damage during missions
4. Col. Eileen Collins; seven, including Col. Collins
5. to deliver supplies and to cooperate in making repairs

Discoveries
1. Share and discuss.
2. National Aeronautics and Space Administration

3. An acronym is a word formed from the first letter or letters of the words being abbreviated. It can usually be pronounced, e.g., UNICEF, OPEC, CD-ROM.

Delving More Deeply
1. STS-114 will test the new tools and procedures that will prevent an accident like the one that destroyed *Columbia* from happening again.
2. STS-114 will prove that the shuttles are flight-worthy. If it fails, NASA will have lost a lot of invested money and time, and national confidence in NASA's programs will decrease.
3. They announce the subject of the article and draw interested readers in to the article.
4. Responses will vary. Share and discuss.

Hidden Depths
1. Responses will vary. Share and discuss. Her comments add another voice to the article, relate NASA's views, and add emotional content.
2. in daily newspapers, in magazines that cover current events, in NASA PR packets, in online news stories

Lesson 25, pages 81–83
On the Surface
1. a
2. six
3. bread, pasta, and potatoes
4. No. Breakfast speeds up metabolism and provides energy.
5. No. It can be dangerous to your health.

Discoveries
1. Share and discuss.
2. Share and discuss.
3. A headline, introductory paragraph, and then columns with headings; it is effective, logical, and easy to read.

Delving More Deeply
1. Responses will vary. Share and discuss.
2. popular, short-term, extreme diets which lack nutrients; examples will vary
3. Consumption should vary with activity and climate; water should not be used as a food replacement.
4. Share and discuss.
5. teenage girls; published in magazine for girls; use of words like "chick"

Hidden Depths
1. The issue of dieting and body image is important to teenage girls and may lead to dangerous eating disorders.
2. Share and discuss issues, e.g., body image, media influence, and so on.

Lesson 26, pages 84–86
On the Surface
1. fifteen
2. Dallas / Ft. Worth
3. Dallas, Ft. Worth, San Antonio, Houston, Austin
4. 7:48 A.M. to Houston Hobby
5. 10:00 P.M.

Discoveries
1. to assist the reader to locate information efficiently
2. estimated time of departure and estimated time of arrival
3. The abbreviations save room and make the schedule quicker to assemble and easier to read.
4. They are listed chronologically by time of departure.

Delving More Deeply
1. These flights are not yet full; some seats are available.
2. It is bad enough to cause delays at the airport.
3. It's impossible to predict everything that might delay a flight, such as weather or technical problems. Likewise, a flight may take less time than expected and arrive early.
4. Perhaps there was a problem with the plane, or perhaps too few commuters wanted tickets for that flight.
5. They can take Flight 136, which leaves 43 minutes later, to Houston Hobby instead.

Hidden Depths
1. Most are traveling to nearby cities for work, not to far-off destinations for work or pleasure.
2. Most probably carry a briefcase or satchel and perhaps a small bag of personal items, because they are not staying at their destinations long.

Lesson 27, pages 87–89
On the Surface
1. Rupa Gomez
2. Sri Lanka
3. She teaches English to migrants.
4. They are sisters.
5. He died during her absence.

Discoveries
1. Share and discuss.
2. Share and discuss.
3. Share and discuss.
4. Share and discuss.

Delving More Deeply
1. In their letters, her relatives pressured her to return.
2. familiarity, pleasure, reaction to sights and sounds of home
3. "Why then did she feel that something — someone was missing?"
4. her mother's black and white sari, a mourning garment
5. Feelings changed from excitement and pleasure to sadness and guilt. Share and discuss evidence and inferences.

Hidden Depths
1. The pleas of her relatives wore down her defenses until she returned home. A battering ram has to have a lot of force behind it to break through castle doors.
2. She means if you move away you can't expect to share in the everyday life of the family. She may be being realistic or may be being vindictive to punish Rupa for her decision to leave.

Lesson 28, pages 90–92
On the Surface
1. Rainforest Action Network (RAN)
2. six
3. rainforestweb.org
4. Randall Hayes
5. E-mail the information to a friend to spread awareness.

Discoveries
1. network, home, rainforestweb.org, e-mail
2. Share and discuss.
3. Share and discuss.

Delving More Deeply
1. Click on the "Action Center" and "Campaigns" sections.
2. "Rainforests"
3. to collect information for schoolwork
4. to represent the main issue or focus of the Web page, and to make it attractive

Hidden Depths
1. Responses will vary. Share and discuss.
2. Responses will vary. Share and discuss.

Lesson 29, pages 93–95
On the Surface
1. Cityside Cinemas
2. between December 5th and 11th
3. ten
4. Share and discuss: General Audience, Parental Guidance Suggested, Parental Guidance Suggested — 13 years and over, Restricted — 17 years and over.
5. four; you can tell by ratings (G or PG)

Discoveries
1. Share and discuss.
2. Share methods.

Delving More Deeply
1. Responses will vary. Share and discuss. The Protector IV, Happy Families, Dance the Night Away, Secret Society, Highway Haze, Shipwrecked, Anna's Quest

2. The Protector IV; it has the greatest number of sessions showing.
3. Secret Society and Lost Cause both have an R rating, and may contain language, images, or ideas unsuitable for children.
4. Share and discuss.

Hidden Depths
1. The Protector IV, Happy Families, Shipwrecked
2. Share and discuss.

Lesson 30, pages 96–98
On the Surface
1. about 115 minutes
2. PG
3. Brad Bird
4. Brad Bird and a writing team
5. A family of superheroes is not allowed to use its powers to help others.

Discoveries
1. He provides the voice talent for a character, Edna Mode.
2. Responses will vary.

Delving More Deeply
1. Harley Michaels
2. It has a great story line.
3. the feature that explains the making of the movie, and the filmmaker's comments
4. the animated short called "Boundin'"
5. the story in "Jack-Jack Attack," which fills in a part of the plot not included in the movie

Hidden Depths
1. Film reviewers must consider how the movie looks, the soundtrack, and the talent of the actors. Both have to consider story and emotional impact.
2. Responses will vary.

Lesson 31, pages 99–101
On the Surface
1. "Harriet's Practice"
2. one month
3. dog biscuits
4. He was bored.
5. searching for food

Discoveries
1. by greeting the guest
2. by thanking the guest
3. They explain who the guest is and what his or her area of expertise or achievement is. At the end, they might sum up the interview and thank the guest.

Delving More Deeply
1. an animal shelter
2. He drops his leash at the man's feet.
3. Responses will vary. Share and discuss.
4. food, going to the park with the man, and watching TV on the couch
5. because he had gotten lost and the man wants him to feel comfortable and that he has his place at home

Hidden Depths
1. Responses will vary.
2. Responses will vary.

Lesson 32, pages 102–104
On the Surface
1. an application for membership at a tennis club
2. so that the member can be contacted wherever he or she is
3. junior, adult, and family
4. Age determines eligibility for membership and price.
5. $150

Discoveries
1. Share and discuss.
2. Share and discuss.
3. Share and discuss.
4. Share and discuss.

Delving More Deeply
1. abide by or follow the "Rules for Members"
2. look after the club and courts, good sportsmanship, wear appropriate clothing, use appropriate language, not lend pass to non-members
3. break rules, not pay fees
4. 86 hours
5. Share and discuss.

Hidden Depths
1. Family would be cheaper at $150. Two juniors would cost $160.
2. to suit members of different ages who play in day and night competitions, and to give the management and staff some time off on weekends

Lesson 33, pages 105–107
On the Surface
1. Kim's mother, Ms. Katy O'Day
2. the principal of Cityside Middle School, Ms. Stern
3. the unhealthy food sold by the school cafeteria
4. No, because the food choices are not healthy
5. raise it at the next PTA meeting

Discoveries
1. formal language and purpose, slightly angry tone
2. Share and discuss.
3. to formalize the complaint and so that she can put forward her argument clearly and logically without interruption

Delving More Deeply
1. No, there is conflict at home about whether Kim may eat in the cafeteria.
2. Yes, it would be convenient since she is a single mother and works long hours.
3. She is pleased with Kim's experience there so far.
4. fresh sandwiches, salads, fruit, yogurt, and fruit juice
5. She knows that the cafeteria needs to make a profit, so it will stock products that are most likely to sell.

Hidden Depths
1. Share and discuss: embarrassed, worried, angry, proud, secretly pleased
2. Responses will vary. Share and discuss.

Lesson 34, pages 108–110
On the Surface
1. sandwiches, muffins, fruit, hot food, yogurt, drinks, sweets, and snacks
2. eleven
3. fruit, yogurt, drinks, and muffins
4. noodles, vegetable soup
5. salad sandwiches, avocado and sprout sandwiches, vegetable soup, carrot muffins

Discoveries
1. Share and discuss.
2. Share and discuss.

Delving More Deeply
1. One is a snack, and the other — frozen yogurt — is more like a dessert. They might be more popular at different times of year — winter and summer.
2. possibly; lower fat, higher fiber, fewer calories if not too large
3. peanut butter sandwich, apricot and almond muffin, chocolate-covered nuts, granola bars
4. They contain high levels of sugar and calories.
5. Soft drinks: They contain empty calories and are high in sugar and caffeine.

Hidden Depths
1. Hot foods, sweets, and snacks; they are easy to prepare, good source of income for cafeteria; students may have wanted them included.
2. Share and discuss.

Lesson 35, pages 111–113

On the Surface
1. bacon, lettuce, and tomato toasted sandwiches
2. five
3. 15 minutes to prepare sandwiches and 5 to cook bacon
4. two
5. seven

Discoveries
1. Responses will vary. Share and discuss.
2. Responses will vary. Share and discuss.
3. Responses will vary. Share and discuss.

Delving More Deeply
1. lunch, dinner, brunch
2. It only takes a few minutes to cook the bacon, but there are several other ingredients to cut, tear, etc., and those processes are more time-consuming.
3. eight
4. It's not necessary but it looks nice and the sandwiches are easier to eat. Presentation is important in food preparation.

Hidden Depths
1. Responses will vary. Share and discuss.
2. low-fat mayonnaise, lean bacon, high-fiber bread

Acknowledgments

The authors and publisher gratefully credit or acknowledge permission to reproduce extracts from the following sources.

ACP Publishing, extract from "Blast Masters" by Joshua Gliddon, *The Bulletin*, 29 October 2002, ACP Publishing: Sydney 2002; Flinders Publishing, extract from "The Mahogany Ship," by Liam Davison, *The Second Largest Island: Modern Australian Short Stories* by Belinda Rickard-Bell (ed.), Flinders Publishing: Maryborough 1994; HarperCollins Publishers, extract from *Take It Personally* by Anita Roddick, Reprinted by permission HarperCollins Publishers Ltd. © Anita Roddick 2001; The Macquarie Library Pty. Ltd., extracts from *Macquarie Dictionary and Thesaurus*, Combined Edition, The Macquarie Library: 1998; Pacific Publications, extract from "Diet myths busted" by Danielle De Gail, *Girlfriend*, September 2002, Pacific Publications 2002; Pan Macmilklan, extract from "Life on Mars" by Werner Von Braun, in *Classic Science Fiction*, by Peter Haining (ed.), Pan: London 1998; Rainforest Action Network, screen capture from *Rainforest Action Network* Web site; Scholastic Australia, extract from *History of Australia* by Manning Clark, Meredith Hooper, and Susanne Ferrier. Text copyright © Manning Clark and Meredith Hooper, 1988. Illustrations copyright © Susanne Ferrier, 1998. Published by Scholastic Australia Pty Ltd, 1988. Reproduced by permission of Scholastic Australia Pty Limited; University of Queensland Press, extract "The Other Country" by Chitra Fernando, in *Beyond the Echo: Multicultural Women's Writing* by Sneja Gunew and Jan Mahyuddin (eds.), University of Queensland Press: St Lucia, 1988; VDL Publications, extract from "I Wish" by Judith Johnson, in *200 Years of Australian Writing: An Anthology from the First Settlement to Today* by JFH Moore (ed.), VDL Publications: Tasmania, 1997.

Every attempt has been made to trace and acknowledge copyright holders. Where the attempt has been unsuccessful, the publisher welcomes information that would redress the situation.